THE NEXT M♞VE
FOR FAMILIES

An Estate Planning Guide
For Parents and Grandparents

Nick Niemann, ESQ

BRIEFBACK
BUSINESS
INSTITUTE

Omaha, Nebraska

Published by:
BriefBack Business Institute LLC
Nick Niemann
1601 Dodge Street
Suite 3700
Omaha, NE 68102
(402) 633-1489
nniemann@mcgrathnorth.com

The Next Move For Families™ trademark is owned by BriefBack Business Institute LLC.

First Softcover Edition 2011

ISBN 10: 0-9796195-2-1
ISBN 13: 978-0-9796195-2-6
Library of Congress Data on file with the publisher.

www.FamiliesNextMove.com
www.OwnersNextMove.com

Printed in the United States of America
10 9 8 7 6 5 4 3

Legal Notice/Disclaimer

Circular 230 Disclosure

Contact Information

Nick Niemann
McGrath North
1601 Dodge Street
Suite 3700
Omaha, NE 68102
(402) 633-1489
nniemann@mcgrathnorth.com

Profile

As a practicing Estate Planning Attorney, Nick Niemann and his team work with families around the country to help them plan and implement their Estate Plans. A properly prepared Estate Plan will help parents and grandparents achieve the personal, family, business and financial legacies they want to achieve.

Nick has advised families for over 30 years and is a frequent speaker at Estate Planning programs around the country. He is also the founder and president of BriefBack Business Institute LLC which publishes Estate Planning guidance for parents and grandparents as well as Transition and Exit Planning guidance for business owners.

Nick is a partner in the Omaha, Nebraska-based national law firm of McGrath North. He has an AV rating from the Martindale-Hubbell National Law Directory (the highest rating for legal ability, ethics, professional reliability and diligence) and has been awarded Lifetime Fellow status by the Nebraska State Bar.

He graduated from Creighton University's College of Business in 1978, summa cum laude, with a degree in accounting and has a CPA certificate. He received his J.D. from Creighton's School of Law in 1981, magna cum laude. While at law school, Nick earned the American Jurisprudence top awards for Estate Planning and for Trusts and Wills. He was also the winner of the Creighton Senior Estate Planning Competition.

He has served on the adjunct faculty of Creighton's School of Law, teaching business owner transition and exit planning, taxation, business valuation and estate planning. He serves on the Trusted Advisor Board for Omaha's Vistage CEO Boards. He also serves on the Headquarters Target Advisory Group and the Small Business Council for the Omaha Chamber of Commerce.

Nick and his wife Ann have been married for over 30 years and have six children and seven grandchildren.

Dedication

This book is dedicated to:

My parents, Ferd and Rita, and my grandparents - for setting the example by taking the right Estate Planning steps to financially protect our families.

My wife, Ann – the love of my life, for being a great wife and a great mother to our six children, Katie, Becky, Christine, David, Lisa and Tricia and a fantastic "Mama Ann" to our grandchildren.

Acknowledgements

I work with an ever increasing number of financial and wealth advisors to assist families with their Estate Planning.

These advisors have long realized that families need to take great care to properly address their Estate Planning needs. I want to thank each of you for trusting me to work with you and your clients to proactively help them to protect themselves and their families.

I also want to thank my partners at McGrath North, with whom I've worked for over 27 years, for the insights, creativity and strategies I've learned from you in assisting families with their Estate Planning.

Nick Niemann

Table of Contents

Introduction to Estate Planning

Introduction To Estate Planning

When Bob and Betty came in to see me, they just wanted to make sure everything was taken care of if something happened to one or both of them. Bob, who had developed a logistics specialization from his time in the military, owned and operated a very successful distribution business. The company had recently extended its business model into an internet-based distribution and fulfillment business.

Betty, who had an MBA from Creighton University, helped in the business by managing their ongoing business model-based strategic planning. She had also handled most of the duties on the home front, in raising their three children – Jack, Joe and Jane. Jack was now married with two children of his own. He was working full time in the business. Joe was in college and hoping to also join the family business. Jane was still in high school.

Bob and Betty were seeking peace-of-mind. They wanted their Estate Planning taken care of. But they weren't sure where to start.

This Guide doesn't pretend to answer all possible questions on Estate Planning. Instead, it is intended to be a quick and easy book to read which will help you to be aware of the principal tools available today to protect yourself, your family and your estate.

Most of all, this book is intended to help you to take a look at your personal, financial and legacy objectives (such as those in the Appendix) and to take the actions you need to take to meet them.

- To Straighten Out
  Misconceptions About
  Estate Planning

- To Show What You:
  - Need To Know
  - Should Do

Chapter 1.   Common Questions

We will start by answering some common Estate Planning questions.

Do I Already Have An Estate Plan?

Everyone has an Estate Plan. The real question is whether your Estate Plan will accomplish what is needed for you and your family.

Most people already have one of the following Estate Plans:

- **A Government Estate Plan** - When you have no Will or Trust, the State statutes control what happens to you upon disability or death and who will receive your Estate. This is known as intestacy.

- **A Simple Will Estate Plan** - This typically leaves your Estate to your spouse and then directly to your children. It requires Probate Court intervention and can waste one of your Estate Tax Exemptions. It also results in distribution to children and grandchildren before they are financially responsible.

- **A Joint Tenancy Estate Plan** - This is when your assets are titled in "joint tenants with rights of survivorship." This means upon your death, your Estate goes to the survivor (generally your spouse). Typically, this results in Probate on the second death and can waste one of your Estate Tax Exemptions. It also doesn't deal with distributions to children and grandchildren after the death of both spouses. This is sometimes used together with a Government Estate Plan or a Simple Will Estate Plan.

- **A Living Trust Estate Plan** - This is the most effective solution being used today. The main feature is a Living Trust (also known as a Revocable Trust), which can be used, among other things, to protect your assets upon your death for your spouse, children and grandchildren, to avoid Probate Court and to obtain the full benefit of both Estate Tax Exemptions.

4

What Is Estate Planning?

Estate Planning means fixing your present Estate Plan to help ensure that:

1. You and your spouse keep control while alive and well;

2. You, your spouse, your children and your grandchildren are protected if you are disabled;

3. You and your spouse have protected your retirement income;

4. Upon your death your spouse, children and grandchildren are provided for and protected;

5. Upon both of your deaths, your property goes to who you want, when you want and how you want; and

6. All of this occurs at the lowest possible tax and other cost to you and your family.

Why Be Concerned With Estate Planning?

It's up to you to have an Estate Plan that protects you, your spouse, your family and your life savings. The failure to do the correct Estate Plan can end up costing a family thousands of dollars in extra probate costs, unnecessary estate taxes, wasted exemptions, investment mismanagement, family disputes, creditor claims and/or child misspending of inheritance funds.

Do I Have An Estate?

You have an Estate if you own any property. Whether your Estate is large or small, it is your Estate. It's up to you to see that whatever amount you have worked to save can be best preserved for your spouse and your family.

What's Included In My Estate?

Your Estate includes the full fair market value of everything you own, such as your:

Home	Life Insurance
Bank Accounts	Real Estate
Household Items	Family Business
Personal Possessions	Family Farm
Stocks & Bonds	Automobiles
Retirement Plans (IRAs, 401(k), etc.)	All Other Assets

When Are My Assets Distributed To
My Spouse After My Death?

If you have a Government Estate Plan or a Simple Will Estate Plan, your assets need to go through Death Probate before being distributed to your spouse. Interim distributions for living expenses can be allowed by the Court.

With a Living Trust Estate Plan, distributions can be made immediately after your death. In addition, typically your spouse is named as the trustee, so that control is maintained.

One of the objectives of Estate Planning is to help your surviving spouse protect your Estate so your resources are available for his or her continued lifetime support.

Unlike a Simple Will, a Living Trust also provides an opportunity to protect funds left to a spouse from the risk of uninsured or underinsured accident claims.

SIMPLE WILL	LIVING TRUST
• Property Received from Husband's Estate Can Be Taken From Wife in Accident Claim	• Property Received from Husband's Estate Can Be Protected From Accident Claims by Spendthrift Provisions of Living Trust

LIVING

TRUST

When Are Our Assets Distributed To Our Children After My Death?

If you have a Government Estate Plan or a Simple Will Estate Plan, then after both of your deaths, and after Death Probate is completed, your assets would be held by a Court-appointed conservator to be used for your minor children (typically until age 21). Children age 21 or older would receive their share, without restrictions, immediately after the Probate, whether or not they are financially responsible.

With a Living Trust, the person you appointed as Successor Trustee (typically a trusted family member or a financial institution) would hold and use your assets for your minor and young adult children to pay for living and education expenses. Final distributions are then typically paid out to them 1/3 at ages 25, 30 and 35 (or whichever ages you choose), when they are more financially responsible (with similar provisions for your grandchildren in case your child has passed away).

Most of my clients agree they don't want their Estates distributed right away in total to their young adult children. Their concern is not only loss or wasting of funds, but also the negative impact that too much money too soon can have on a child. The Simple Will offers no means to solve this. The Living Trust does.

SIMPLE WILL	LIVING TRUST
• No Protection for Children or Grandchildren Inheritance • Risk Loss Due to Misspending, Creditors, Marital Disputes, Divorce • Less Appreciation for What They've Received	• Children and Grandchildren Inheritance Protected • Distributed Over Time • Investments Professionally Managed • Children and Grandchildren Learn to Appreciate What They've Received • You've Left Instructions That Will Benefit Your Children and Grandchildren Long After You've Gone

What Is A Disability Probate?

If you become disabled and you don't have Financial and Health Care Powers of Attorney, then your family goes to Probate Court, and the following happens.

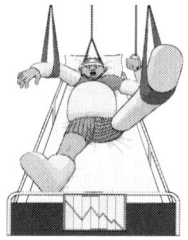

1. The **Court picks** a person to act as your Conservator to handle your financial matters and a person to act as your Guardian to handle your medical matters.

2. The **Court supervises** this Disability Probate for as long as you are disabled.

There is a cost involved to set this up and then annually report back to the Court for as long as you are disabled.

This can be estimated as follows:

Cost Estimate

Average Legal Costs To Set Up	$ 3,000
Average Annual Costs ($1,200/Year Estimate)	7,200
6 Year Illustration	$10,200

What Is Death Probate?

Death Probate is a public court process your family goes through upon your death of proving your Will, paying your creditors and distributing to your heirs the assets titled in your name at death. It typically takes 1-2 years.

The cost of going through this depends on the complexity of your Estate and the State in which you are a resident.

A national study found the average cost to be as follows:

Estate Size	Probate Cost
$ 100,000	$ 5,000
200,000	9,900
300,000	14,700
400,000	19,600
500,000	22,500
600,000	26,880
700,000	31,220
800,000	35,520
900,000	39,780
1,000,000	44,000
1,500,000	65,250
2,000,000	86,000
3,000,000	126,000
4,000,000	164,000
5,000,000	200,000

SOURCE: National Underwriter Field Guide, based on actual government studies

What Is The Federal Estate Tax?

The Federal Estate Tax is explained in more detail in The New Federal Estate Tax chapter. The Federal Estate Tax is a tax -- usually paid on the death of the surviving spouse based on the value of all assets in your Estate. Under the Federal tax laws as they exist for 2011 and 2012, each parent is eligible for a Lifetime Exemption (something I refer to as a "coupon"). Under this the first $5,000,000 of your Estate is exempt. This means that a married couple can exempt $10,000,000 of their Estate if their Estate Plan is properly set up to receive both exemptions (i.e. both coupons).

What Is Joint Tenancy?

CAUTION
JOINT TENANTS AHEAD

- Joint Tenancy is joint-ownership of an asset.
- Upon death, the asset goes 100% to the survivor.

Joint Tenancy Can Be A Poor Alternative:

Between Spouses
- Does Not Eliminate Probate on 2nd Death.
- Doesn't Allow for Specified Distribution to Children and Charities.
- Could Forfeit All or Part of the Benefit of One of the Federal Estate Tax Lifetime Exemptions (your tax exemption "coupons").

Between Parent & Child
- Could Lose Your Assets To Child's Creditors or Ex-Spouse.
- Survivor Takes All – May Conflict with Equal Shares to all Children.

Chapter 2. What Do Most People Want To Accomplish

Like most parents and grandparents, Bob and Betty had a number of items they wanted to accomplish. I find that most people want to accomplish some or all of the following results from Estate Planning. Place an ☒ by those items you want to accomplish.

☐ Peace of Mind.
☐ Protect & Keep Control of My Assets While I or My Spouse Are Alive.
☐ Protect & Keep Control of My Assets If I or My Spouse Are Disabled.
☐ Provide Clear Direction & Authority About Medical Care for Me & My Spouse.
☐ Plan for Nursing Home Care Costs.
☐ Treat My Children Equally.
☐ Help My Favorite Charity.

☐ Protect My Estate For My Children & Grandchildren.
☐ Avoid Unnecessary Estate & Income Taxes.
☐ Avoid Unnecessary Wasting of My Estate by My Children & Grandchildren.
☐ Avoid Unnecessary Probate Expenses.
☐ Avoid Family Disputes About My Estate.

To Make Sure My Life Savings Go To Whom I Want, When I Want

 and

Probate Court

Dept. of Revenue

Spendthrift

IRS

Con Man

To Make Sure My Life Savings Don't Go To Those I Don't Want To Have It

Disgruntled Heirs

Former In-Law

Nursing Home

Probate Attorney

Chapter 3. Problems To Be Overcome

One of the main purposes of Estate Planning is to help avoid or solve certain problems that almost every family will encounter or need to deal with. These can be divided into the following 5 areas:

ASSET WASTE & MISMANAGEMENT

- Waste of assets by children or grandchildren receiving inheritance before they are financially responsible
- Family disputes due to failure to leave proper financial instructions
- Inability to sell your family business when you want at a full, fair price
- Inadequate investment management by your survivors
- Risk of your assets coming under control of a surviving spouse's next spouse
- Failure to provide for Long-Term Care costs

TAXES

- Federal Estate Taxes
- State Inheritance Taxes
- Double Estate/Income Tax on Retirement Plans
- Estate Taxation of Life Insurance Proceeds
- Loss of all or some of the benefit of your Estate Tax Lifetime Exemption
- Loss of your $13,000 Annual Gift Tax Exemptions

FAMILY NEEDS

- Inadequate funds (such as life insurance) to support spouse and dependents after your death
- Insufficient instructions for care and custody for minor children after your death
- Court picked guardians for minor children
- Failure to provide for special needs children
- Improper healthcare directives

ACCIDENT/LAWSUIT RISKS

- Claims on your children's inheritance by former spouses
- Exposing your assets to your children's or grandchildren's creditors
- Lawsuit expenses and jury awards from underinsured or uninsured business or personal accidents or injury
- Business partner disputes

PROBATE

- Death Probate can cost up to 4-5% of your Estate
- Multiple Death Probates if you have real estate in another State
- Probate on the death of the surviving spouse for couples who rely on joint tenancy
- Disability Probate costs and hassles if you become disabled

Many of these concerns were expressed by Bob and Betty. Steps for addressing these are covered throughout this Guide.

Chapter 4. What's The Size Of My Estate?

Before going any further, you should estimate the size of your Estate. While most of the discussion in this Guide will apply regardless of the size, you'll have a better idea of what additional tools and techniques are needed and available to you if you know the size of your Estate.

You have an Estate if you own any property. Your Estate includes the value of everything you own, which you can estimate as follows:

ASSETS	ESTIMATED VALUES			
	Husband	Wife	Joint	Total
Home	$_____	$_____	$_____	$_____
Bank Accounts	$_____	$_____	$_____	$_____
Household Items	$_____	$_____	$_____	$_____
Personal Possessions	$_____	$_____	$_____	$_____
Stocks & Bonds	$_____	$_____	$_____	$_____
Retirement Plans	$_____	$_____	$_____	$_____
Life Insurance (Policy Amount)	$_____	$_____	$_____	$_____
Real Estate	$_____	$_____	$_____	$_____
Family Business	$_____	$_____	$_____	$_____
Family Farm	$_____	$_____	$_____	$_____
Automobiles	$_____	$_____	$_____	$_____
Other Assets _____	$_____	$_____	$_____	$_____
_____	$_____	$_____	$_____	$_____
_____	$_____	$_____	$_____	$_____
_____	$_____	$_____	$_____	$_____
TOTAL ASSETS	$_____	$_____	$_____	$_____

LIABILITIES				
	Husband	Wife	Joint	Total
Home Mortgage	$_____	$_____	$_____	$_____
Other Debts _____	$_____	$_____	$_____	$_____
_____	$_____	$_____	$_____	$_____
_____	$_____	$_____	$_____	$_____
_____	$_____	$_____	$_____	$_____
TOTAL LIABILITIES	$_____	$_____	$_____	$_____

NET WORTH
Assets - Liabilities = Net Worth $_____ $_____ $_____ $_____

Chapter 5. Main Estate Planning Options

Estate Planning today includes choosing from the best available tools and techniques to help in overcoming the above problems and to accomplish what you need and want to do. Below are the main options that apply to most clients in the following situations.

These are accomplished by executing a Basic Estate Plan that has these documents:

- Will
- Living Trust
- Financial Power of Attorney
- Health Care Power of Attorney
- Healthcare Directive
- Estate Planning Letter

If You Own Any Property

☐ If you die without a Will, the State Statutes specify who receives your separate property. In Nebraska, generally only $100,000 plus 1/2 of the balance of your property goes to your spouse. The balance goes directly to your children. Having a Will or Living Trust enables you to specify who receives your property.

If You Are Married

☐ After your death, your Living Trust can hold, manage and/or distribute your Estate for your spouse. It can also help protect your Estate for your spouse against certain unforeseen liability, accident, creditor and litigation risks. You and your spouse control all aspects of your Living Trust.

If You Want To Keep Control Upon Your Disability

☐ A Financial Power of Attorney and Health Care Power of Attorney enable your spouse and/or other selected family member or friend to manage your financial and health care matters for you if you become disabled - without the need for costly Court conservatorship intervention or supervision.

☐ A Health Care Directive (Living Will) can avoid useless, extraordinary medical procedures in a terminal condition.

If You Have Children

☐ If you have minor children, your Will can name your hand-picked guardian and avoid Court-appointed conservator/guardianship proceedings after your deaths. Your Estate Planning Letter can specify child raising instructions for the guardian you selected.

☐ If you have minor children, your Living Trust can hold your family investments after your deaths, to pay for minors' living expenses (without Court conservatorship intervention).

☐ If you have school age children, your Living Trust can continue to hold your family investments after your deaths as one pool to benefit all children until the youngest graduates, so the younger children receive equal treatment and aren't required to use up their share on their education.

☐ To avoid inheritance misspending, your Living Trust can hold your family investments when your children are minors and continue as they become young adults, then distribute each child's share over time as they become financially responsible (e.g. 1/3 at ages 25, 30 & 35).

☐ Your Living Trust can also help protect your family investments from your childrens' creditors and your childrens' potential marital disputes.

☐ If you have or expect grandchildren, and if your child dies, your Living Trust can continue to hold and protect that child's share in trust for the grandchildren.

☐ Your Living Trust can also include family incentive and disincentive provisions in which distributions are tied to specified child/grandchild accomplishments or other suitable conditions.

If You Want to Designate Last Wishes

☐ Your Estate Planning Letter can designate funeral and burial wishes.

☐ Your Estate Planning Letter can designate who receives selected personal property or momentos.

To Do List

√ _____
√ _____
√ _____
√ _____
√ _____

Chapter 6. Other Estate Planning Options

Depending on your family, your objectives and your financial situation, other Estate Planning Options may be recommended to overcome other problem areas. Below are some of the tools and techniques being commonly used today. Place an ⊠ by those items you want to accomplish.

If You Own Life Insurance

☐ If your Estate exceeds $5,000,000 ($10,000,000 if married), then about 35% of your Life Insurance must be paid for Estate Taxes. With a Life Insurance Trust, these taxes can normally be avoided and your Life Insurance can be fully preserved for your family.

If You Want To Avoid Probate Court

☐ On your death, property separately titled in your name must go through Probate Court before distribution to your family, taking 1-2 years and costing additional Probate Court legal fees. If before death you re-title your property to your Living Trust, you avoid Probate Court.

If Your Estate Exceeds $5,000,000

☐ After the deaths of both spouses, Federal Estate Taxes (at about 35%) are due. A married couple with a Simple Will or Joint Tenancy Estate Plan receives only one $5,000,000 exemption (unless the portability election is made, as discussed in The New Federal Estate Tax chapter). A Living Trust can be used to obtain the full benefit of a second $5,000,000 Estate Tax Exemption (total $10,000,000 exempt). Spouses should balance ownership between themselves to help assure each spouse has sufficient property so both exemptions can be used.

☐ Property gifted during your life to children and grandchildren is not subject to your Estate Tax. You and your spouse can each gift (tax free) up to $13,000 per child/grandchild per year (Annual Exemption Gifts). You can also use all or part of your $5,000,000 Lifetime Estate Tax Exemption during your lifetime if you wish. So, you and your spouse can choose to each gift (tax free) up to $5,000,000 over your life (Lifetime Exemption Gifts).

☐ Investments held in a Family Limited Partnership or Limited Liability Company can be used as a way to make your Annual Exemption Gifts and your Lifetime Exemption Gifts and to reduce Estate Taxes.

If You Want To Keep Some Control Over Gifts

☐ A Gift Protection Trust, Family Limited Partnership or Limited Liability Company can be used to make your Annual Exemption Gifts and your Lifetime Exemption Gifts. These can also hold your gifts for your minor and young adult children and grandchildren to make distributions over time as your children financially mature. These can also help protect gifts from children misspending, children's creditors and children marital disputes.

If You Own A Business

☐ A Business Owner Transition Growth Plan (also known as a Succession Plan or Exit Plan) can be used to provide a proactive plan for keeping your business interest protected and growing and to help you transition from it or sell it in an orderly fashion. It can specify buy-out conditions, retirement options, and stock price, as well as limit Estate Taxes. It can also preserve ownership and management amongst your family or partners or arrange for sale of your business. See my website for business owners which covers this topic further. www.OwnersNextMove.com.

If You Own Investments

☐ A Family Limited Partnership or Limited Liability Company can help protect your investments from unforeseen liability, accident, creditor and litigation risks.

To Do List

√ _____
√ _____
√ _____
√ _____
√ _____

Estate Planning For Families With All Size Estates

Estate Planning For Families With All Size Estates

Due to their desire to protect their growing family, Bob and Betty needed to address a number of areas. They wanted to be certain that each spouse and the children were protected in the event of either's death or disability.

Because of changes to Federal and State laws over the past 30+ years, and due to development in the Estate Planning profession, the choices available today for Bob and Betty — and for you - to solve Estate Planning issues are much more extensive than in the past.

YOUR MAIN CHOICES IN THE PAST	YOUR MAIN CHOICES TODAY
ESTATE PLANNING	**ESTATE PLANNING**
Will Trust	Pour Over Will Living Trust Estate Planning Letter Financial Power of Attorney Health Care Power of Attorney Healthcare Directive (Living Will) Family Limited Partnership Life Insurance Trust Buy-Sell Agreement Limited Liability Company Family Private Foundation Asset Protection Trust Etc.

However, key to accomplishing anything great is to take the first step. That's where the Basic Estate Plan comes in. It takes 2 appointments to accomplish this. One to review your needs. The second to execute the documents.

The documents we include in the Basic Estate Plan may be all that you need or want to do. Indeed, many clients find this is all they

19

need to do. For that reason, what follows is a discussion of the 6 documents we include in most Basic Estate Plans. This is recommended for small, medium, and large Estates, as well as for simple and complex Estates. Later in this Guide is a discussion of additional choices for large estates and special situations and objectives.

It's important that all parents and grandparents "begin with the end in mind". We all want to protect our families. Let's start at the beginning and let's be certain that we do not overlook even the most obvious situations.

Where To Begin?
(for all Parents and Grandparents –
Small Or Large Estates)

First Step In Famous   =   **"Catch Rabbit"**
Rabbit Stew Recipe

Don't Overlook The Obvious

To Do List

√ _____

√ _____

√ _____

√ _____

√ _____

Chapter 7. The Estate Plan Portfolio

What Do You Include In Most Basic Estate Plans Today?

Our Basic Estate Plans today will normally include the following tools. Each of these are specifically designed to help parents to protect certain financial and health care needs for their families.

ESTATE PLAN PORTFOLIO

Prepared for

Bob A. Parent
And
Betty A. Parent

Prepared By:
Nick Niemann

McGrath, North, Mullin & Kratz, PC LLO
Attorneys At Law
1601 Dodge Street
Suite 3700
Omaha, NE 68102

Phone: 402-341-3070
Fax: 402-341-0216

1. LAST WILL

2. LIVING TRUST

3. ESTATE PLANNING LETTER

4. FINANCIAL POWER OF ATTORNEY

5. HEALTH CARE POWER OF ATTORNEY

6. HEALTHCARE DIRECTIVE (LIVING WILL)

Your Estate Plan Portfolio is your OWNER'S MANUAL

BOB A. PARENT and BETTY A. PARENT
Estate Plan Portfolio

1. LAST WILL	Your Last Will distributes assets still titled in your name to your Living Trust after your death. It appoints your Executor and a guardian for any minor children.
2. LIVING TRUST	Your Living Trust enables you to keep control of your assets during your life, lets your successor trustee manage them if you become disabled, and either distributes them to your spouse, children or other heirs at your death or holds them in trust till a later date. When separate Living Trusts are used for each spouse, this can be used to obtain the lifetime estate tax exemption for each spouse. This Trust can be used as either a Standby Living Trust (which standing alone doesn't avoid Probate) or as a Funded Living Trust (to reduce or avoid Probate).
3. ESTATE PLANNING LETTER	This contains directions to your trustee and family on the distribution of selected personal items. It lists your wishes with regard to burial and funeral. It contains an Information Organizer, record of insurance and retirement plans, and list of key advisors and friends to be contacted.
4. FINANCIAL POWER OF ATTORNEY	This document lets you appoint a selected person (such as your spouse or adult child) to manage your financial affairs if you become mentally or physically disabled.
5. HEALTH CARE POWER OF ATTORNEY	This document lets you appoint a selected person (such as your spouse or adult child) to make important health care decisions if you become mentally or physically disabled.
6. HEALTHCARE DIRECTIVE (LIVNG WILL)	This document provides authorization to your physician regarding the use or nonuse of extraordinary medical procedures or life support in the event of a serious illness.

Chapter 8. Your Last Will

Your Last Will is used to name your executor (personal representative) of your Estate and the guardian of your minor or disabled children.

Your Will also deals with most assets not owned by your Living Trust. It is designed to work together with your Living Trust. You can use your Living Trust as either a Standby Living Trust or as a Funded Living Trust. With a Standby Living Trust, title to your assets is not transferred to your trust during your life (therefore, the trust is not used for reducing or avoiding the probate court process). After your death, your Will transfers any remaining assets titled in your name to your Living Trust.

With a Funded Living Trust, title to your assets is transferred to your trust during your life, which avoids probate on these assets.

Therefore, the Last Will operates as a Pour Over Will, because it ultimately pours over your non-trust assets after death into your Living Trust, to be held or distributed according to your wishes, as stated in your Trust.

You can convert your Standby Living Trust to a Funded Living Trust (and therefore avoid probate) by titling your assets to your Living Trust any time before death. As a safeguard to help avoid probate, the agent you have appointed in your Financial Power of Attorney can have the authority to transfer property into your Trust before your death if you are unable to do so (which converts your Standby Living Trust to a Funded Living Trust).

POUR OVER WILL

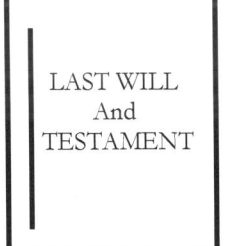

LAST WILL
And
TESTAMENT

AFTER YOUR DEATH:

- Appoints Guardian for Any Minor or Disabled Children
- Appoints Your Executor (Personal Representative)
- Transfers Any Remaining Property to Your Living Trust Upon Your Death

Chapter 9. Your Living Trust

Your Living Trust is the key safety and protection component of your Estate Plan. So I like to illustrate it as a safe. You keep the "combination" to your Safe while you are alive and well. You appoint successors to have the "combination" upon your death or disability.

Your Living Trust is designed to accomplish the following:

During Your Lifetime:

- You manage and have total control over the assets of the Trust during your life.
- You can amend or revoke your Trust any time for any reason.
- You can add property to, or take property out of, your Trust at any time.
- Protects against conservatorship proceedings (or Disability Probate) if you become legally incompetent or disabled.

After Your Death:

- Distribute your assets to your spouse, children or other heirs as you've directed or continue to hold your assets in trust for certain beneficiaries (such as minors, young adults, grandchildren and spendthrifts) until an age or ages when they are financial responsible. For example, the trust can hold all assets in a pool for the benefit of all children until the youngest is 22 (i.e. graduates from college) then split into equal shares for each child, distributing 1/3 at ages 25, 30 and 35.
- Avoid or substantially reduce Estate Taxes, depending on the size of your estate, by obtaining the Lifetime Estate Tax Exemptions for both spouses for married couples.
- Avoid Death Probate for all assets and property transferred to the Trust during your life.
- Receive all assets probated after your death from your Will that were not transferred to the Trust during your life.
- Receive all life insurance and retirement plan proceeds where you've named the Trust as the beneficiary.
- Reduce the risk of a will contest and court challenges to your Estate Plan.

SUMMARY OF A LIVING TRUST

A Living Trust is created simply by signing the Trust Agreement prepared by your Estate Planning Attorney. The Trust will refer to some terms you might not be familiar with. These are summarized below:

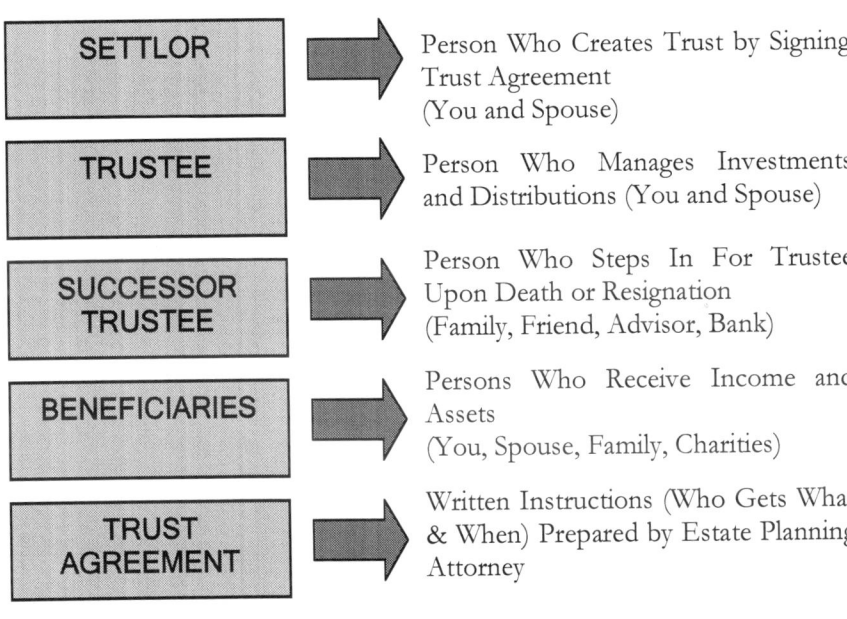

SETTLOR	Person Who Creates Trust by Signing Trust Agreement (You and Spouse)
TRUSTEE	Person Who Manages Investments and Distributions (You and Spouse)
SUCCESSOR TRUSTEE	Person Who Steps In For Trustee Upon Death or Resignation (Family, Friend, Advisor, Bank)
BENEFICIARIES	Persons Who Receive Income and Assets (You, Spouse, Family, Charities)
TRUST AGREEMENT	Written Instructions (Who Gets What & When) Prepared by Estate Planning Attorney

---

LIVING TRUSTS

Wall Street Journal: • "The advantages of Living Trusts over Wills are considerable."

   • "Living Trusts have become the preeminent modern estate planning tool."

Readers Digest: • "The Living Trust is the finest gift a husband can give his wife."

THE STANDBY LIVING TRUST

When you sign your Living Trust, you have created a Standby Living Trust. In essence, the Trust is now "standing by", ready to receive whatever assets you re-title into it.

When you re-title your assets into the name of your Living Trust, you have now "funded" it, so it becomes a Funded Living Trust.

Many people decide to not yet take the added steps now to fund their Living Trust, but instead just leave their trust as a Standby Living Trust. They can always fund it later. As long as you do this before death, Probate can be avoided. If you become disabled before death, the person appointed under your Financial Power of Attorney can fund your Living Trust for you before death.

The Standby Living Trust has all of the advantages of a Funded Living Trust and will accomplish for you all of the same objectives as a Funded Living Trust except for one - the Standby Living Trust doesn't avoid Probate. If you die with a Standby Living Trust, your Will needs to be filed in Probate Court and your property will be distributed to your Living Trust, to be held in trust or distributed to your family as you provided - but Probate is needed to accomplish this.

Therefore, if you wish to avoid Probate, you should "fund" your Living Trust before death (by re-titling your assets to it).

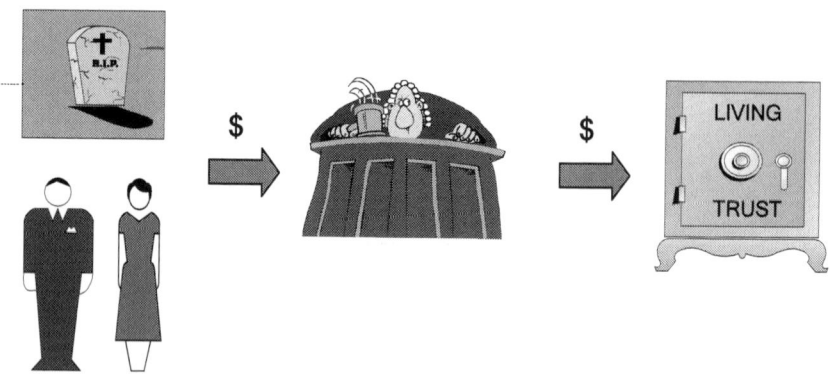

THE FUNDED LIVING TRUST

If You Want to Avoid Probate

In Nebraska, your Estate must go through Probate if it is larger than $30,000 real estate or $50,000 of personal property. Other states require Probate at different levels.

Following execution of your Living Trust and other Estate Plan documents of your Basic Estate Plan, you now have the option -- should you choose to take advantage of it -- to avoid Probate on all or part of your Estate. This can be done by transferring ownership (i.e. title) of your assets to your respective Living Trusts. To the extent that title is in the name of your Living Trusts upon death, then those assets do not need to go through Probate Court. In other words, you can convert your Standby Living Trust into a Funded Living Trust by re-titling your assets to your Living Trust while you're alive.

Many people choose not to implement this option until later in life and are willing to take the chance that they will have an opportunity prior to death to transfer title to their Living Trusts. This is your choice. As a fallback, we can provide in your Financial Powers of Attorney that the Agent you have appointed under the power of attorney has authority to transfer title to your Living Trusts. This could be useful, for example, if you were to have a period of disability prior to death, which would enable your Agent to assist in putting these types of matters in order before death.

If you choose not to transfer title to all of your assets to your Trust for now, then upon your death, those assets in your name (other than Joint Tenant with Rights of Survival assets and those assets with different beneficiary designations) would pass under your Will, through Probate Court, to your Trust, to be distributed as your Trust directs.

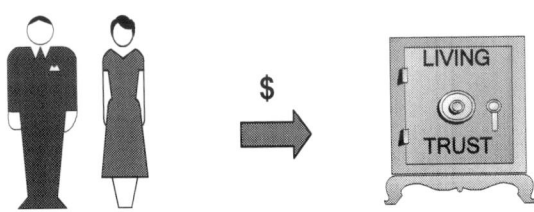

HOW DO YOU RE-TITLE YOUR ASSETS TO YOUR LIVING TRUST?

To re-title your assets to your Living Trust (i.e. to turn it into a Funded Living Trust), the following documents must be executed:

ASSET	ASSET RE-TITLING DOCUMENT	FUNDED LIVING TRUST
Home	→ Deed	→
Bank Accounts	→ Bank Account Re-Title Letter	→
Household Items	→ Household Items Assignment	→
Personal Possessions	→ Personal Possessions Assignment	→
Stocks & Bonds	→ Stock or Bond Power	→
Retirement Plans	→ Change of Beneficiary	→
Life Insurance	→ Change of Beneficiary	→
Real Estate	→ Deed	→
Family Business	→ Assignment of Assets	→
Family Farm	→ Deed	→
Automobile	→ Title Assignment	→

To Do List

√ _____

√ _____

√ _____

√ _____

√ _____

COMPARING THE SIMPLE WILL TO THE LIVING TRUST

Features	Simple Will	Standby Living Trust	Funded Living Trust
Your Disability – Upon your disability, holds and manages your assets to avoid Disability Probate.	No	Yes	Yes
Spouse Distributions – Upon your death, distributes protection for your Spouse.	Yes	Yes	Yes
Spouse Protection – Can hold assets in trust for liability protection for your Spouse.	No	Yes	Yes
Child Fairness – Upon death of both Spouses, holds assets as one pool until youngest child reaches age 22 or graduates (where applicable).	No	Yes	Yes
Child Equal Shares – Upon death of both Spouses, divides assets into equal shares based on number of children.	Yes	Yes	Yes
Child Living Expenses – Holds shares in trust, but distributes principal and income as needed.	No	Yes	Yes
Investments – Allows designation of professional investment manager.	No	Yes	Yes
Asset Protection – Protects assets from child's creditors or marital disputes.	No	Yes	Yes
Financially Responsible – Final distributions to children at designated ages, e.g. 1/3 at ages 25, 30 and 35, when children are financially responsible.	No	Yes	Yes
Estate Tax Deferred – No Estate Tax till death of both Spouses.	Yes	Yes	Yes
Estate Tax Exemptions – Obtains full use of both Federal Lifetime Estate Tax Exemptions.	No	Yes	Yes
Death Probate – Avoids Death Probate.	No	No	Yes
Charities – Can designate charitable bequests.	Yes	Yes	Yes
Other – Potentially several other features mentioned in the Estate Planning Guide.	No	Yes	Yes

Typical Simple Will Estate Plan

Period #1 – Both Bob & Betty Parent Living

Bob Parent Will
Executor: Betty Parent

- Retain complete control of Assets until disability
- Disability Probate or Conservatorship if disabled

$

- Can be amended or revoked until death
- No change in income taxes

Period #2 – After Death of Bob Parent

$

- All property goes to Betty outright
- Must go through Probate Court
- Executor: Betty Parent
- Beneficiary: Betty Parent

$

- None of the property grows estate tax free
- None of the property protected from creditors
- All principal and income used as needed.

Period #3 – After Death of Betty Parent

$

- Must go through Probate Court
- Property divided into equal shares based on number of children
- Children still in school must pay education and living expenses out of their share
- Property for minor children must be managed by Probate Court in a Conservatorship

$

- Property for young adult children (age 21+) is distributed outright, even if they are not yet financially responsible.
- No protection of assets from child's creditors or marital disputes
- No provision to hold in trust for grandchildren in case child dies
- No designation of professional investment manager

Features
- Subject to both Disability and Death Probates
- No Estate Tax till death of Betty Parent
- Full benefit of only one Lifetime Estate Tax Exemption

30

Typical Living Trust Estate Plan

Period #1 – Both Bob & Betty Parent Living

Bob Parent Living Trust
Settlor: Bob Parent
Trustee: Bob Parent
Beneficiary: Bob Parent

• Retain complete control of assets
• Avoids "Disability Probate" or
  conservatorship

$

• Can be amended or revoked
  until death
• No change in income taxes

Period #2 – After Death of Bob Parent

↓ **$ BALANCE**

Up to $5,000,000 ↓

Marital Trust
Executor: Betty Parent
Beneficiary: Betty Parent

Family Trust
Executor: Betty Parent
Beneficiaries: Betty Parent
                and Children

• May distribute to Betty
  Parent as needed
• Betty Parent may terminate
  Trust and hold assets
  personally (unless QTIP)

• Grows estate tax free
• Protected from creditors
• Principal and income used
  as needed for living, education
  and health expenses

Period #3 – After Death of Betty Parent

$

Family Trust

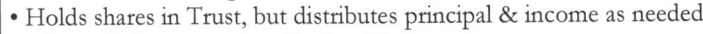

• Held as one pool until youngest child reaches age 22
• Then divided into equal shares based on number of children
• Holds shares in Trust, but distributes principal & income as needed
• Allows designation of professional investment manager
• Protects assets from child's creditors or marital disputes
• Final distribution to children at stated ages, e.g. 1/3 at ages 25, 30, 35
• If child predeceases (or dies before e.g. age 35) child's share held in
  trust for grandchildren till designated ages (e.g. 1/3 at ages 25, 30, 35)

$

Features
• No Disability Probates
• No Death Probates if Funded Living Trust
• Assets Protected for Children and Grandchildren
• No Estate Tax till death of Betty Parent
• Full benefit of both Lifetime Estate Tax Exemptions

COST OF SIMPLE WILL vs. LIVING TRUST

A Simple Will can be less expensive on the front end. But the use of it means you and your family will incur higher costs later (e.g. due to Death Probate). The Living Trust gives you the opportunity to plan your Estate to avoid or minimize the other future costs covered in this Guide.

SIMPLE WILL   LIVING TRUST

But the Cup is $10.00   Including the Cup

INVESTMENT ADVISOR DESIGNATION

Most parents have developed a good relationship with an investment adviser they know and trust. You've come to realize a good investment adviser will help you achieve a better annual return on your investments and will also help you avoid making bad investment choices and losing your principal. However, when you are gone, the last thing you want is for your children (or your selected Successor Trustee) to take on investing without professional help. For this reason, you can include in your Living Trust an Investment Advisor Designation.

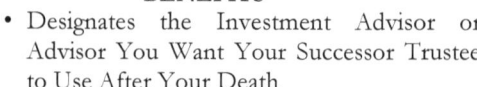

BENEFITS

- Designates the Investment Advisor or Advisor You Want Your Successor Trustee to Use After Your Death
- Provides Continuity of Your Investment Plans With the Person You Already Trust
- Can Be Designated in Your Living Trust

EXAMPLE:

$500,000 Investments

ASSUMPTION: The right advisor will add 4% +/- higher average annual return (better returns and/or less losses) due to better investment selection.

RESULT: 10 Year Additional Growth = $200,000

32

BENEFICIARY DESIGNATIONS

When you have a Living Trust, you can name the Trust as beneficiary of your Life Insurance and Retirement Plans so that these dollars funnel through the Trust and are held in Trust or distributed according to your overall Estate Plan. This also enables you to avoid Probate on these funds. (Typically your Spouse is primary beneficiary of retirement plans, and your Trust is secondary - for income tax reasons).

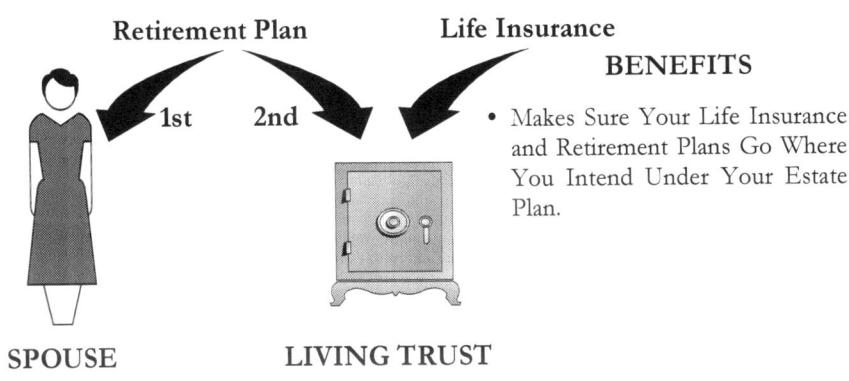

Retirement Plan   **Life Insurance**

1st   **2nd**

BENEFITS

- Makes Sure Your Life Insurance and Retirement Plans Go Where You Intend Under Your Estate Plan.

SPOUSE   **LIVING TRUST**

SPOUSE ASSET EQUALIZATION

By balancing asset ownership amongst spouses, you reduce the risk of loss if a spouse incurs a substantial, uninsured accident claim, a business loss indemnity or guarantee obligation or other uninsured claim. In addition, a Living Trust by itself will not assure that you receive the full benefit of both Federal Estate Tax Exemptions if the first spouse to die doesn't have property titled in his or her name at least equal to half of your combined estates (up to the Lifetime Estate Tax Exemption amount). The new portability provision of the new Federal Estate Tax does not cover value growth after the death of the first spouse, so ownership balance remains important.

BENEFITS

- Makes Sure You Receive Both Lifetime Estate Tax Exemptions Regardless of Who Dies First.
- Potential Asset Protection Upon Accident or Disability Claim.

QTIP PROVISIONS

The Living Trust can also include provisions (known as QTIP provisions) to help address the following 2 marriage situations. If your first spouse has died and you are remarried, you might be hesitant to leave your Estate outright to your second spouse, if you or your children have a concern your second spouse might disinherit your children. Yet you still want your Estate to provide support for your second spouse. A QTIP provision can do this and still assure that your children inherit the remainder after your second spouse's death.

A QTIP provision can also be useful in a second situation. If you are concerned your first spouse might not protect your assets after your death if your surviving spouse remarries, a QTIP provision can support your surviving spouse and assure your children inherit the remainder.

BENEFITS

- **Second Marriage Situation**. Assures Your Assets Go To Children of First Marriage.
- **Remarriage Situation**. Protects Your Assets for Your Children After Your Death if Surviving Spouse Remarries.

SPECIAL NEEDS SUB-TRUST

If you have a special needs child, you realize that special steps need to be taken to provide for the care, health and well-being of your child. Your Living Trust can help, by including a Special Needs Sub-Trust. This is not suitable in all cases, but when it applies, it can enable you to still provide protected funds for your child without disqualifying government funded health and living expense programs.

BENEFITS

- Enables Parents to Address Special Financial Needs of Disabled Children.

EDUCATION SUB-TRUST

Most couples want to leave their Estate equally to their children. However, where some children have had more of their own children than their siblings have had, you may wish to provide a separate share to help pay for your grandchildrens' education. Your Living Trust can include special provisions to set-aside part of your Estate specifically for the education costs of your grandchildren.

BENEFITS

- Allocate Part of your Estate for Grandchild Education.
- Can Do Without Using Your Child's Share of Your Estate.

CHARITABLE BEQUEST

While most people will set aside certain amounts for charitable donations during their life, many also like to make additional donations upon their death as part of their Estate Plan. Either your Living Trust or a Will can be used to make charitable bequests.

BENEFITS

- Helps Your Favorite Charities.
- Can Easily Be Included In Your Will or Living Trust.
- Estate Tax Savings.

ONE OR TWO LIVING TRUSTS

Depending on the size of your Net Worth, we will suggest whether you need a Living Trust for each Spouse or whether you can both use the same Living Trust. With the increase of the Lifetime Estate Tax Exemption to $5,000,000 per person, those couples who expect their Net Worth to be less than $5,000,000 may be able to just have one Living Trust.

Other Estate Planning considerations may impact this decision, such as asset protection desires to keep your assets balanced between spouses or a need to reflect separate ownership of inherited assets.

New $5 Million Exemption
Favors Needing Only One

Chapter 10. Your Estate Planning Letter

The Estate Planning Letter is optional for you, but you may wish to fill it in to help your family with the following areas:

- Instructions for Gifts of Personal Items After Your Death

- Burial and Funeral Wishes

- Checklist of Actions to Take After a Death

- Information Organizer

- Key Advisors to be Contacted

- Relatives and Close Friends to be Contacted

- Record of Life Insurance Policies

- Record of Disability and Long-Term Care Insurance Policies

- Record of Retirement Plans

- Family Information and List of Your Property

- Instructions for Raising Your Children After Your Death

ESTATE PLANNING LETTER

- **Directs Gifts of Special Personal Items.**

- **Funeral Instructions.**
- **Church and Other Services.**

- **Cemetery – Burial Wishes.**
- **Specifies Whom Memorials Go To.**
- **Other Instructions.**

Chapter 11. Your Financial Power of Attorney

If you should become disabled, through illness or accident, and be unable to take care of your financial affairs, your spouse or family member would need to file for a Disability Probate with the local Probate Court, to request to be appointed as the Conservator to handle your financial matters. During the continuance of your disability, the Conservator would need to periodically file a report with the Court regarding your earnings and expenses.

Your Financial Power of Attorney enables you to avoid that. This document relates to your financial affairs. It lets you name an Agent (such as a spouse or other family member) to look after your property and financial affairs on your behalf if you are disabled and unable to make those decisions on your own.

This document also authorizes your Agent to transfer title to your property to your Living Trust. Property transferred to your Living Trust will be managed by your Trustee. Property not placed in the name of your Living Trust will be controlled while you are living, but disabled, by your Agent acting under this Financial Power of Attorney.

FINANCIAL POWER OF ATTORNEY

BENEFITS

- Appoints A Person to Handle Your Financial Affairs If You Become Disabled.
- Avoids A Disability Probate or Conservatorship.

EXAMPLE:

Cost Estimate – Disability Probate $10,000
(6 Year Illustration)

Savings $10,000

Chapter 12. Your Health Care Power of Attorney

In addition to needing to address financial matters if you become disabled, you also need to address health care matters.

Without a power of attorney, in order to approve and direct health care matters for you, your spouse or family member may need to file for a Disability Probate to request to be appointed as your Guardian to handle and authorize your health care matters.

Your Health Care Power of Attorney enables you to avoid going to Court. This document relates to your health care matters. It enables the person you designated as your "Agent" (such as your spouse or other family member) to make health care decisions for you if you become disabled and are unable to make those decisions for yourself.

We typically suggest that you name one or more successors to your initial Agent in case of the death or resignation of your initial Agent.

HEALTH CARE POWER OF ATTORNEY

BENEFITS

- Appoints A Person to Make Medical Decisions for You If You Become Disabled.
- Avoids A Disability Probate or Guardianship.

Chapter 13. Your Health Care Directive (Living Will)

Your Health Care Directive (also known as a Living Will) provides direction to your physician and hospital for dealing with major, life threatening illnesses and injuries if you become unable to make decisions for yourself.

Under State law, a physician or hospital may be legally required to perform useless, extraordinary medical procedures unless you have directed otherwise in a Health Care Directive.

This document is intended to work in conjunction with your Health Care Power of Attorney - however it accomplishes the added step of providing a legal directive directly to your physician to carry out your wishes - rather than just authority to your Agent under your Health Care Power of Attorney. This enables your Agent to work more closely with your physician.

You should furnish a signed original copy of the Living Will to your physician or health care provider.

HEALTH CARE DIRECTIVE
(Living Will)

BENEFITS

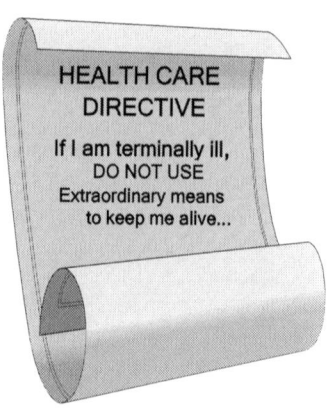

HEALTH CARE DIRECTIVE

If I am terminally ill, DO NOT USE Extraordinary means to keep me alive...

- A Directive to Your Physician for Dealing With Life Threatening Illnesses and Injuries.
- Avoids the Need for Court Intervention.

NOTE:

- Proper Limiting Standards to Address Moral Considerations.

AVOIDING DISABILITY PROBATE

The combination of the Living Trust, Financial Power of Attorney, Health Care Power of Attorney and Health Care Directive (Living Will) give you the means to successfully avoid a Disability Probate if you become disabled.

This enables you to keep such matters private rather than engaging an Attorney and Probate Court Judge to be involved in a personal disability.

DISABILITY PROBATE

(No Powers of Attorney)
- Spouse Needs to Go to Probate Court to Handle Financial and Health Care for Disabled Spouse.

NO DISABILITY PROBATE

LIVING TRUST

FINANCIAL POWER OF ATTORNEY

HEALTH CARE POWER OF ATTORNEY

HEALTH CARE DIRECTIVE

- Spouse Can Take Care of Financial and Health Care for Disabled Spouse.

Husband   Wife   Attorney   Judge

Husband   Wife

Chapter 14. Executing Your Basic Estate Plan

SO, NOW WHAT DO I DO?

So, now you realize an Estate Plan is critically important, not only for you and your spouse, but also for your children and grandchildren. So you've decided you want to actually get this done. What do you do? It's a 4 step process:

4 STEPS:

1. Set up Appointment With Your Estate Planning Attorney
2. Meet For About 1 ½ - 2 Hours
   - Fill Out and Bring Estate Planning Appointment Form
3. Your Estate Planning Attorney Will Prepare and Send You A Draft
4. Follow-Up Appointment to Sign Your Estate Plan
   - You'll receive 2 sets of signed documents – one for home, one for safekeeping elsewhere (such as a safe deposit box)

Professionals working together produce the best and most effective Estate Plans. Experienced investment advisers, financial planners, accountants, and life insurance advisers understand the benefits and importance of Estate Planning. After all, they spend years helping you grow your investments, save income taxes, reduce family expenses and provide insurance coverage. The last thing they want to see is their efforts go to waste because you failed to execute an Estate Plan. So, most Estate Plans get done because one of them has referred you to an Estate Planning Attorney.

Your Estate Planning Attorney typically will work with that adviser to help decide what Estate Planning options are best suited for you based on your family, your objectives and your financial situation.

WHO ELSE HELPS SET UP YOUR ESTATE PLAN?

- **Investment Adviser**
- **Financial Planner**
- **Accountant and/or**
- **Life Insurance Adviser**

Team Approach
Working Together With Estate Planning Attorney

Your Appointment Form.

As an Estate Planning Attorney I will send you in advance of your Appointment a form to fill in and bring with you, which summarizes certain family and financial information. This page and the next page show the form we use:

BASIC ESTATE PLAN

FAMILY AND FINANCIAL INFORMATION

FAMILY INFORMATION

	Husband or Single	Wife	Child Names	Age	M or S	City/State	# Kids
Name:			1.				
Address:			2.				
City/State/Zip:			3.				
Phone:			4.				
Age:			5.				
Soc. Sec. #:			6.				
State of Residency:			Any Special Child/Grandchild Health Concerns:				
Citizenship:							
Employers:							
Health Concerns:			Other Comments:				
Prior Marriages?							
Prior States:							

FINANCIAL INFORMATION

ASSETS	HUSBAND or SINGLE	WIFE	JOINT
Home	$	$	$
Bank Accounts	$	$	$
Household Items	$	$	$
Personal Possessions	$	$	$
Stocks & Bonds	$	$	$
Retirement Plans	$	$	$
Life Insurance (Policy Amt.)	$	$	$
Real Estate	$	$	$
Family Business	$	$	$
Family Farm	$	$	$
Automobiles	$	$	$
TOTAL	$	$	$
LIABILITIES			
Home Mortgage	$	$	$
Personal Debts	$	$	$
Other Liabilities	$	$	$
TOTAL	$	$	$
NET WORTH			
Assets-Liabilities = Net Worth	$	$	$

OTHER ADVISERS

Investment/Financial Adviser:	
Life Insurance Adviser:	
Accountant:	
Family Physician:	
Other:	

McGRATH NORTH MULLIN & KRATZ, PC LLO

Suite 3700 First National Tower   Attorneys at Law
1601 Dodge Street   Phone: (402) 341-3070
Omaha, NE 68102-1627   Fax: (402) 341-0216

Website: www.mcgrathnorth.com

Chapter 15. Answers To 10 Common Estate Planning Objections

Sometimes a spouse or family member may offer some objections to Estate Planning, with the result that nothing gets done. Below are our Answers to 10 of the more common objections we've heard:

1. **"I Don't Have Time"**. An appointment takes only about 1½ to 2 hours.

2. **"I Don't Want To Assemble A Lot Of Information"**. A short information summary is used to prepare your basic Estate Plan. Most people can answer this off the top of their head.

3. **"I'm Too Young"**. You are old enough unless you can predict when you will die or become disabled.

4. **"It's Too Confusing For Me"**. Your Estate Planning Attorney will spend the time to explain Estate Planning simply and understandably.

5. **"I Don't Know What To Do"**. Most people aren't sure what to do either. Your Estate Planning Attorney will explain and suggest exactly what you should do.

6. **"I Don't Know The Cost"**. Your Estate Planning Attorney can normally quote you a fee up front.

7. **"My Family Doesn't Need This"**. A well done Estate Plan is the best way to maintain peace in the family after a disability or death.

8. **"The Government Will Take Care Of Us"**. The government doesn't provide you with a good Estate Plan.

9. **"My Family Will Get Everything Anyway"**. Minus unnecessary Estate and Income Taxes, Probate costs, Estate dispute costs, creditor claims, and inheritance misspending.

10. **"I Already Did An Estate Plan Years Ago"**. Are you sure it was done right? Is it up-to-date? Have your adult children protected the property you are giving them by doing their own Estate Plan?

Chapter 16. Two Types Of Estates After Death

Since we also handle settling and distribution of Estates after a death, we've seen all types of Estate Plans. You can actually group them all into 2 categories. Which do you want to be in?

As parents, we are always working to set a good example for our children and grandchildren. How we set up our Estate Plan is one of those opportunities to set a great example.

Whether good or bad, this is an example which will be remembered for a long time by our families. Did we leave them a mess or did we leave them peace-of-mind.

CLEAN UP	CLEAN
• Incorrect or Outdated Estate Plan.	• Correct Up-To-Date Estate Plan.
• Tax and Financial Matters Not In Order.	• Tax and Financial Matters In Order.
• No Peace-of-Mind.	• Peace-of-Mind.
• Costly and Time-Consuming to Settle and Distribute Estate After Death.	• Relatively Easy to Settle and Distribute Estate After Death.

Chapter 17. Times For Estate Plan Check-Up

Is your present Estate Plan correct for your present situation? Is it up-to-date? When should you have an Estate Plan Check-Up?

We typically recommend a check-up in the following 12 situations:

MARRIAGE

FIRST CHILD

RESIDENCY CHANGE

EVERY 4-5 YEARS

DIVORCE

MAJOR HEALTH CHANGE

SECOND MARRIAGE

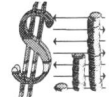

MAJOR ESTATE $ CHANGE

LAW CHANGE

RETIREMENT

NURSING HOME

FAMILY DEATH

To Do List
√ _____
√ _____
√ _____
√ _____
√ _____

ESTATE PLAN CHECK-UP

The following is a list of some of the main Estate Plan Check-Up actions you need to take or consider upon each of these 12 life events. Place a ☐ by those items you need to address or wish to discuss.

Marriage

☐ Revise Estate Plan to add Spouse as beneficiary.
☐ Name Spouse as new appointee for Financial Power of Attorney and Health Care Power of Attorney.
☐ Acquire Life Insurance and Disability Insurance to provide for spouse and children.
☐ Sign Estate Planning Letter.

First Child

☐ Revise Estate Plan to add child as beneficiary.
☐ Designate Guardian for child in your Will.
☐ Increase Life Insurance and Disability Insurance.
☐ Revise Estate Planning Letter for Child Care.

Residency Change

☐ Revise Estate Plan to meet requirements for new State.
☐ Consider impact of new State's estate and inheritance tax.
☐ If expecting to sell certain investments or business consider if this is best before or after residency change, to manage income tax impact.

CALENDAR

Every 4 – 5 Years

☐ Revise Estate Plan due to changes in desired appointees for your Living Trust (trustees), Will (Executor/Personal Representative), Financial Power of Attorney (Agent), Health Care Power of Attorney (Agent) .
☐ Revise persons (families, charities, etc.) or times you desire for distributions from your Living Trust upon your death (in order to best protect or provide for your family).
☐ Establish or modify your education funding.
☐ Establish or modify your charitable bequests.
☐ For business owners, adopt, review or revise your Transition Growth Plan (aka Succession Plan or Exit Plan).
☐ Make sure you have titled your assets to your Living Trust.
☐ Update life, disability and long-term care insurance.
☐ Make sure life and disability insurance and retirement plan beneficiary designations are up-to-date and correctly name your Living Trust where applicable.
☐ Review retirement projections with financial advisor.
☐ Confirm assets are appropriately balanced between spouses.
☐ Make sure Life Insurance Trust is being properly kept up.
☐ Confirm your adult children's Estate Plans are handled.
☐ Update your Personal Asset Protection Plan.

Divorce

☐ Revise Estate Plan where spouse had been named as appointee or beneficiary.

☐ Revise Estate Plan to adjust coverage for children.

Major Health Change

☐ Revise Estate Plan to provide for special needs.

☐ Make sure persons named as appointees to address your financial and health care issues are informed.

☐ Make sure Health Care Power of Attorney and Health Care Directive are current.

☐ Make sure Financial Power of Attorney is current.

Second Marriage

☐ Revise Estate Plan to name Spouse and address other matters which arise from a second marriage.

☐ Revise Estate Plan to address yours/hers children situations.

Major Estate $ Change

☐ Revise Estate Plan to address changes to plan for distribution of estate.

☐ Address Estate and Gift tax planning strategies.

☐ Address investment management needs.

Law Change

☐ Address revisions to Estate Plan due to estate, trust and health care law changes.

☐ Address new tax planning due to tax law changes.

Retirement

☐ Determine pre-Nursing Home planning to address assets to be utilized for care.

☐ Review retirement plan elections.

☐ Update Estate Planning letters (e.g. for gifts of personal items and funeral wishes).

Nursing Home

☐ Determine Nursing Home, assisted living or home care alternatives and costs.

☐ Revise appointees under Living Trust, Will, Financial Power of Attorney and Health Care Power of Attorney.

☐ Update Health Care Directive (Living Will).

Family Death

☐ Address post-death estate and trust asset transfers, Federal and State estate tax returns, county inheritance tax return, post-mortem elections and tax planning, post-death income tax returns and determination if Death Probate is needed.

☐ Revise Estate Plan of surviving spouse due to changes in desired appointees for your Living Trust (trustees), Will (Executor/Personal Representative), Financial Power of Attorney (Agent), Health Care Power of Attorney (Agent).

☐ Revise persons or times you desire for distributions from surviving spouse's Living Trust upon death.

Chapter 18. Your Adult Children Estate Plans

Are you now finished? Maybe. Maybe not. You've taken a huge step and accomplished a lot by executing your Basic Estate Plan. You've seen to it that your Estate is preserved for your spouse, children and grandchildren.

But have your young adult children done what they should to preserve their inheritance for their families. Some parents and grandparents give their children or grandchildren as a Birthday, Anniversary or Christmas gift an Estate Plan from their Estate Planning Attorney.

However you choose to handle it, we believe a valuable parental suggestion to your children or grandchildren is they should take care of their own Estates, as you have done for them.

BENEFITS

Helps Assure:

- Your Children and Grandchildren Don't Waste the Inheritance and Gifts You Left Them
- Your Children Preserve Their Estate For Their Children

To Do List

√ _____

√ _____

√ _____

√ _____

√ _____

Chapter 19. Your Personal Asset Protection

We live in a litigious society. It is generally prudent to protect your hard-earned assets through certain asset protection tools. These types of tools can protect your investment and other assets against unwarranted and unexpected, but potential, creditor  claims, which may arise, for example, from business operations, personal accidents, personal injury, or other casualties and contingencies. The following is a partial list of personal asset protection planning tools which you should consider:

- **Avoid or Remove Personal Guarantees.** During the course of life, you may have been asked to sign a personal guarantee on debts of your children or siblings or of your business. The removal of your personal guarantees should be sought whenever possible.

- **Irrevocable Trust.** When investment assets are transferred out of your name as a gift to a family member, then those assets are not subject to your personal risk. Gifted assets would typically, however, be subject to the personal liability risk of the individuals who received your gift. By transferring investment and/or life insurance assets into an irrevocable trust for the benefit of your children or grandchildren, you can remove the assets from your personal exposure. By placing spendthrift provisions in the trust, you can also protect these assets from the personal liability exposures of your children and grandchildren.

- **Asset Balance Between Spouses.** Both spouses typically have a certain amount of potential liability exposure (e.g. due to personal accidents). However, typically, the spouse who is active in business has a greater level of potential creditor claims. By balancing your assets between the two spouses, you can minimize the risk of a more substantial loss of assets than if your net worth is entirely in the name of the spouse who is most subject to liability exposure.

- **Investment Protection Entities.** Just as you can place a business operation into a corporate entity to shield yourself from those business risks, you can also place your investment assets into certain types of limited partnerships, limited liability companies, and asset protection trusts, in order to shield those assets from your business and personal risks. Under these types of entities, a litigation judgment against you can typically not be collected against the assets of the asset protection partnership or trust. Asset protection partnerships, LLCs or trusts established in the United States may provide a certain degree of protection. Due to more favorable laws enacted by some countries, a foreign asset protection trust may provide higher degree of protection, although it also costs a significant amount more to implement and its effectiveness has been challenged in recent years.

- **Proper Insurance Coverage Mix.** The proper mix of business and personal casualty insurance protection, along with business and personal umbrella insurance should be implemented and periodically reviewed, depending on changing business operations and personal situation.

- **Business Owners.** If you own a business, certain additional asset protection steps should be taken. See my website for business owners for more detail. www.OwnersNextMove.com.

Estate Planning For Families With Larger Estates

Estate Planning For Families With Larger Estates

The success of Bob and Betty's company, combined with reasonable cumulative returns on their personal investments, had enabled Bob and Betty to grow a significant net worth which now exceeded $10 million and was expected to continue to grow into the future.

While the Basic Estate Plan generally should be executed for most families, certain other additional Estate Planning tools and techniques are designed specifically to help solve situations that exist for families having a larger net worth.

What follows are several Estate Planning tools and techniques which we reviewed with Bob and Betty and which are commonly used today for families having a larger financial net worth. Included are certain financial calculations to illustrate the impact.

ALL ESTATES	ESTATES OVER $50,000	ESTATES OVER $5,000,000
YOU NEED ALL OF THESE: • Last Will • Living Trust • Estate Planning Letter • Financial Power of Attorney • Health Care Power of Attorney • Health Care Directive	**YOU ALSO NEED THIS:** • Funded Living Trust	**YOU USUALLY ALSO NEED ONE OR MORE OF THESE:** • Proper Marital Deduction • Family (Credit Shelter) Trust • Spouse Asset Equalization • Family Annual Exemption Gifting • Family Lifetime Exemption Gifting • Gift Power of Attorney • Family Limited Partnership (or LLC) • Life Insurance Trust • Grantor Retained Annuity Trust • Intentionally "Defective" Grantor Trust • Estate Tax Payment Life Insurance • Family Private Foundation • Generation Skipping Exemption Trust

Chapter 20. The New Federal Estate Tax

In December 2010 Congress re-enacted the Federal Estate, Gift and Generation–Skipping Taxes for 2010, 2011 and 2012. The key features of the new tax law relevant to our discussion in this Guide include the following:

- The Estate, Gift and Generation-Skipping tax rates have been re-unified at the same top rate of 35%.
- The Lifetime Estate Tax Exemption is raised to $5,000,000.

- The Lifetime Gift Tax Exemption is raised to $5,000,000 (which can be used at any time during your life. To the extent you use it, your Lifetime Estate Tax Exemption is reduced).

- If a spouse dies without fully needing or using the Lifetime Estate Tax Exemption, the unused amount can be used by the surviving spouse at his or her death. This is known as the portability provision.

- The Lifetime Generation Skipping Tax Exemption is raised to $5,000,000.

Summary of New Federal Wealth Transfer Taxes

	2009	2010	2011	2012
•-------------------------------------- Estate Tax---•				
Exemption	$3.5 million	Elect $5 million or no estate tax	$5 million (with portability)	$5 million, indexed (with portability)
Max Tax Rate	45%	35%	35%	35%
Basis Step-Up at Death	Unlimited	Elect unlimited or $1.3 million + plus $3 million spousal	Unlimited	Unlimited
•--------------------------------------Gift Tax---•				
Lifetime Exemption	$1 million	$1 million	$5 million (portability)	$5 million, indexed (portability)
Max Tax Rate	45%	35%	35%	35%
•-------------------------------Generation Skipping Tax-------------------------------•				
Lifetime Exemption	$3.5 million	$5 million	$5 million (w/o portability)	$5 million, indexed (w/o portability)
Max Tax Rate	45%	35%	35%	35%

The future of these provisions beyond 2012 is uncertain. The Obama Administration proposed budget released February 14, 2011 would raise the Estate Tax rate to 45% and would lower the Exemption from $5 million per person to $3.5 million.

Chapter 21. Family Annual Exemption Gifting

Property gifted during your life to children and grandchildren is not subject to your Estate Tax. You and your spouse can each gift (tax free) up to $13,000 to each child/grandchild each year (Annual Exemption Gifts). The gifted amount and the future appreciation on the gifted amount avoids Estate Taxes.

	Don't Gift	Gift & Use Exemption
Stock Value Today	$13,000	$13,000
Stock Value in 10 Yrs (at Death)	23,000	23,000
Estate Taxes Saved per Gift	$ -0-	$ 8,050

Whether or not you should gift involves more than just tax considerations. The first question is whether you are comfortable with the amount you'll have left after gifting. The second question is whether you are comfortable with your children or grandchildren receiving financial gifts. The third question is choosing which assets to gift. If you own stock in a family corporation, that stock is often an ideal asset to gift (provided certain steps are taken to deal with voting and control over stock ownership). If you own marketable securities (stocks and bonds), one of the best ways to gift a portion of these is to place them into a Family Limited Partnership (or a Limited Liability Company) and then gift shares of that.

If you decide to begin a gifting program, we'll often recommend you sign a Gifting Power of Attorney so your program can be continued even if you become disabled.

ANNUAL GIFTING PROGRAM

BENEFITS

Up to $13,000 per Parent, per Child, Each Year

- Tax Law Allows a $13,000 Gift to Each child and Grandchild Each Year
- Each Gift Saves About $4,550 in Future Estate Taxes
- Also Avoids Tax on the Growth in Value. For example, if the $13,000 gifted property grows in value to $23,000 at your death, you've saved about $8,050 Estate Tax.
- Family Limited Partnership, LLC and Children's Trust are Popular Tools to Use to Make Gifts

57

Chapter 22. Family Lifetime Exemption Gifting

Each spouse is entitled to a $5,000,000 Lifetime Estate Tax Exemption. You can use all or part of your $5,000,000 Lifetime Estate Tax exemptions either during your lifetime or at death. You can use it during your lifetime by making gifts to your family members up to $5,000,000. The advantage of using the exemption during your lifetime is that the exempt amount - plus post-gift value appreciation - is all removed from your taxable estate.

The use of just $1,000,000 of your $5,000,000 during your life can be illustrated as follows:

	Don't Use Until Death	Use Today
Stock Value Today	$1,000,000	$1,000,000
Stock Value in 10 Yrs (at Death)	1,800,000	1,800,000
Value of Exemption	1,000,000	1,800,000
Estate Taxes Saved (at 35%)	$ 350,000	$ 630,000

In this example, by not using the exemption until death, it was worth only $1,000,000 and saved $350,000. However, by using the exemption today, the $1,000,000 avoids Estate Tax on whatever the value of today's gift is worth at your death. In this example, the $1,000,000 stock grew to $1,800,000 by death. So, the exemption saved $630,000 in Estate Tax. The use of the full $5,000,000 during your lifetime would result in $3,150,000 of added estate tax savings in the above example.

LIFETIME GIFTING PROGRAM

Up To
$5,000,000
per
Spouse

BENEFITS

- You Can Use All or Part of Your $5,000,000 Exemption During Your Life - Rather Than Waiting Till Death
- Benefit is NO ESTATE TAX ON ALL Future GROWTH in Value of the Gift
- Family Limited Partnership, LLC and Children's Trust are Popular Tools to Use to Make Gifts

Chapter 23. Family Limited Partnership

A partnership is a legal entity your attorney creates for you by filing a Certificate of Limited Partnership with the Secretary of State and having you and your spouse sign a Partnership Agreement. This is much like incorporating your business. The difference is you form a partnership instead of a corporation and you put investments into it instead of a business. This provides a number of benefits partially illustrated below.

If you own your investments directly in your name or your Living Trust, they are taxable at full fair market value.

If instead they are held in a Family Limited Partnership (FLP) or Limited Liability Company (LLC), they can be value-discounted to reduce Estate Taxes.

	Investments in Your Name	Investments in FLP or LLC
Gross Investment Value	$1,000,000	$ 1,000,000
Less e.g. 25% Discount	-0-	-250,000
Taxable Value	$1,000,000	$ 750,000
Estate Taxes	350,000	262,500
Estate Taxes Saved	-0-	$ 87,500

Many clients want to begin gifting to save taxes, but also want to maintain some control over gifted funds. An FLP or LLC can provide this control by holding your gifts for your children and grandchildren.

You can direct distributions over time or as your children/grandchildren financially mature. These can also help protect gifts from children/grandchildren misspending, children's/grandchildren's creditors and children/grandchildren marital disputes.

In addition, you can gift more because investments gifted this way can be value-discounted to increase the tax benefit of your Exemption Gifts.

To be effective for Estate and Gift tax purposes, the partnership (or LLC) will include certain provisions to qualify for the Annual Exemption Gifts as a "present interest" and to avoid Federal Estate Tax by certain limits on control.

Family Limited Partnership (or LLC)

	Outright Gift	Gift in FLP or LLC
Gross Investment Value	$13,000	$17,333
Less e.g. 25% Discount	-0-	-4,333
Annual Exemption Gift	$13,000	$13,000
Extra Property Gifted Tax Free Per Gift		$ 4,333

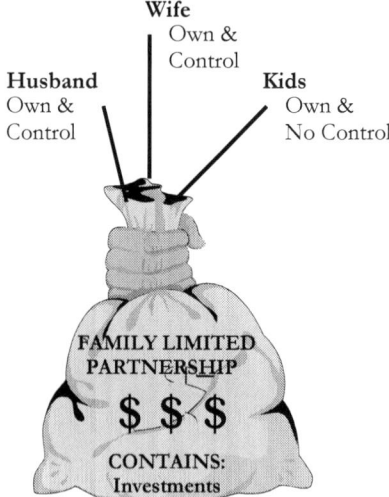

Wife
Own & Control

Husband
Own & Control

Kids
Own & No Control

FAMILY LIMITED PARTNERSHIP

$ $ $

CONTAINS:
Investments

BENEFITS

- **Income Tax Savings**
- **Estate Tax Savings**
- **Gift Tax Savings**
- **Asset protection**
- **Maintain Certain Controls**
- **Teach Financial Responsibility to Kids**
- **Flexible**

Chapter 24. Life Insurance Trust

If you own Life Insurance and your Estate exceeds the Lifetime Estate Tax Exemption ($5,000,000 each, $10,000,000 if married), then about 35% of your Life Insurance proceeds (over the exemption amount) must be paid for Estate Taxes if you own the Life Insurance policy or if your Estate is the beneficiary. With an Irrevocable Life Insurance Trust ("ILIT"), these taxes can be avoided and your Life Insurance can be fully preserved for your family.

	No ILIT	With ILIT
Life Insurance Amount	$1,000,000	$1,000,000
Estate Tax on Insurance	-350,000	-0-
Net After Tax	$650,000	$1,000,000

Why is this? The reason is that if you own the Life Insurance policy or if your Estate is the beneficiary, then the proceeds (face value) of the Life Insurance will be subject to Estate Taxes.

You can avoid this by gifting the policy to someone else or, as to new policies, set up ownership somewhere else (so it's not in your Estate).

But who should you gift it to? Who should own your life insurance? If your spouse owns it, it will still be subject to you and your spouse's Estate Tax. If your children own it directly, then you've defeated the purpose of holding your Estate in trust until they reach certain ages. Plus, if they own it, the proceeds can't easily be used for the benefit of your surviving spouse. If your Living Trust owns it, the proceeds will still be subject to Estate Tax.

The most frequently used solution is to sign a Life Insurance Trust. This is used to avoid Estate Tax on your life insurance. This Trust will have provisions essentially the same for holding and distributing to your children, and it also holds the funds for the benefit of your surviving spouse.

The Life Insurance Trust needs to be both the owner and beneficiary of the life insurance policy (and should also be the policy applicant for new policies). Premiums are paid with funds that you annually place in the trust. If you provide certain specific withdrawal rights to the trust beneficiaries (e.g. your children), then the premium payments can qualify for your Annual Exemption Gifts.

To be tax-effective, the Trust itself needs to be irrevocable because it in essence is a gift of the policy to your beneficiaries. However, the Trust has enough flexibility that this typically poses no problem.

Life Insurance Trust

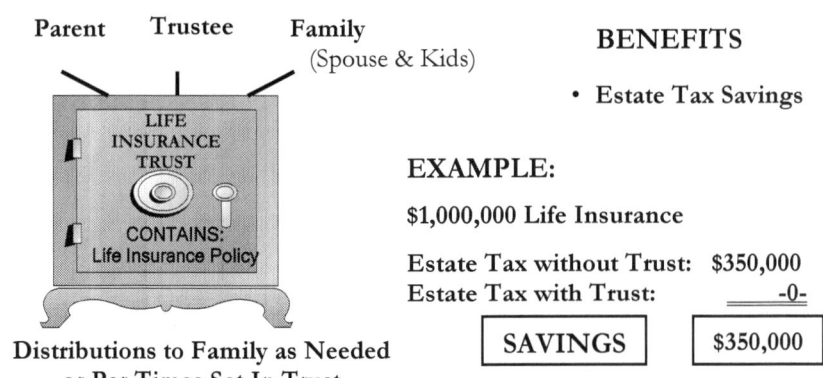

BENEFITS

• **Estate Tax Savings**

EXAMPLE:

$1,000,000 Life Insurance

Estate Tax without Trust:	$350,000
Estate Tax with Trust:	-0-

SAVINGS	$350,000

Parent   Trustee   Family
                    (Spouse & Kids)

LIFE INSURANCE TRUST

CONTAINS:
Life Insurance Policy

Distributions to Family as Needed or Per Times Set In Trust

Chapter 25. Grantor Retained Annuity Trust

If your present Net Worth exceeds the Lifetime Estate Tax Exemption ($5,000,000 each, $10,000,000 if married), and you wish to implement an Estate Tax savings tool to complement an Annual Exemption gifting program, the Grantor Retained Annuity Trust ("GRAT") offers a valuable option.

The GRAT works like this. You establish the GRAT by executing a specific type of trust agreement. Next you transfer property (e.g. cash, investments or company stock) to the trust. The trust provides you with an agreed annuity payment each year. When the trust is set up so that the net present value of this annuity is at least equal to the value of the property you transferred to the trust, then you have a net taxable gift of zero.

To the extent that the property you transferred to the GRAT grows in value at a higher rate than the interest rate the IRS requires to be used in calculating the net present value of the annuity (generally about 1% higher than the rate for IDGTs), you will have transferred a net gift to the beneficiaries of your GRAT without a gift tax.

This can be illustrated as follows (using a 6% annual growth rate):

	Value Today	Value In 10 Years
Property Transferred	$3,000,000	$ 5,370,000
Annuity Value	- 3,000,000	- 4,030,000
Net Gift	-0-	
Net Value Passed To Heirs (Tax Free)		$ 1,340,000

Grantor Retained Annuity Trust

2011   2015 – 20 +/-

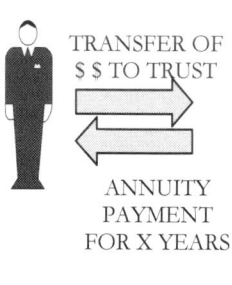

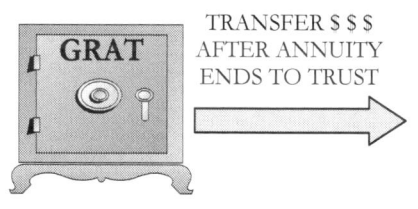

TRANSFER OF $ $ TO TRUST

TRANSFER $ $ $ AFTER ANNUITY ENDS TO TRUST

ANNUITY PAYMENT FOR X YEARS

Benefit: Move Most of 2 – 10 Year Growth Out of Owner's Estate

Chapter 26. Intentionally "Defective" Grantor Trust

If your present Net Worth exceeds the Lifetime Estate Tax Exemption ($5,000,000 each, $10,000,000 if married), and you wish to implement an Estate Tax savings tool to complement an Annual Exemption Gifting program, the Intentionally Defective Grantor Trust ("IDGT") offers a valuable option.

The IDGT works like this. You establish the IDGT by executing a specific type of trust agreement. Next, you transfer "seed" capital to the IDGT, generally in an amount equal to at least 10% of the overall transaction (this is a gift which needs to be covered by use of a gift tax exemption).

Next you transfer the property you intend to gift to the IDGT in exchange for a Promissory Note equal to the value of the property. This results in a net gift of zero (so no use of a gift tax exemption is needed).

This technique works when the property you gifted to the IDGT grows in value at a rate higher than the interest rate on the Promissory Note. The IRS has rules which establish from time to time the minimum interest rate you must charge (generally about 1% lower than the rate required for GRATs). The growth in the value in excess of the interest you receive on the Note is removed from your Estate and goes to the benefit of your heirs.

This can be illustrated as follows (using a 6% annual growth rate):

	Value Today	Value In 10 Years
Property Transferred	$3,000,000	$ 5,370,000
Promissory Note	- 3,000,000	3,660,000
Net Gift	-0-	
Net Value Passed To Heirs (Tax Free)		$ 1,710,000

This trust is called "defective" because, while it is considered effective at removing the investments from your estate for estate tax purposes, you still own them for income tax purposes. This "defect" actually works to your benefit, because your payment of the income tax on the trust income is an allowable tax-free gift to your beneficiaries.

Intentionally "Defective" Grantor Trust

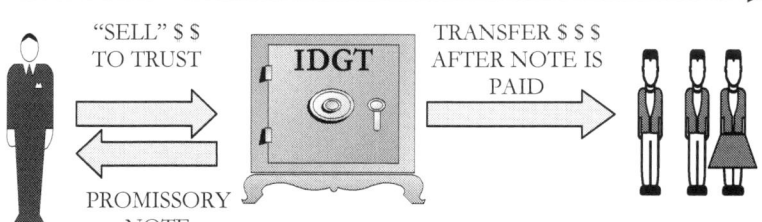

Benefit: Move Most of
5 – 10 Year Growth Out
of Owner's Estate

Chapter 27. Family Private Foundation

Everyone is motivated to make gifts to charity for a variety of reasons. Depending on your objectives, various techniques exist to not only meet those objectives, but to also achieve substantial tax savings at the same time. The Family Private Foundation is one such popular approach.

This is a charity set up for you by your Estate Planning Attorney which you control. It can hold your tax deductible cash or investment contributions and distribute them over time to other charities. It can also avoid capital gain taxes and investment income taxes. It can also avoid the combined Estate and Income Taxes on Retirement Plan accounts. It can become a charitable program your children can continue.

	Keep For Family	Give To Foundation
Retirement Plan	$1,000,000	$1,000,000
Estate & Income Taxes	- 500,000	-0-
What's Left	$ 500,000	$1,000,000

This approach also enables you to transfer funds into the Foundation today, claim a tax deduction this year for the entire contribution, but pay the funds out to charity over several years as you determine to do so. Only a 5% minimum needs to be paid out of the Foundation each year.

FAMILY PRIVATE FOUNDATION

Husband
Control
Till Death

Wife
Control
Till Death

Kids
(Control After Parents Deaths)

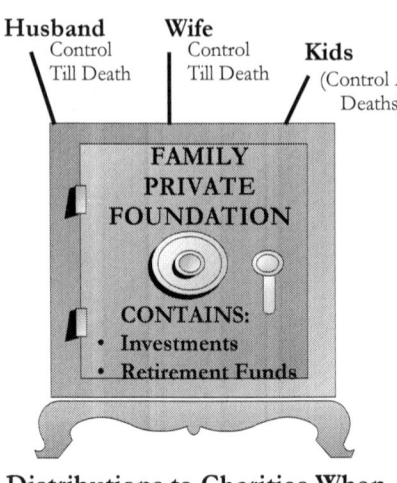

FAMILY
PRIVATE
FOUNDATION

CONTAINS:
• Investments
• Retirement Funds

Distributions to Charities When You Want

BENEFITS

• Income Tax Savings
• Estate Tax Savings
• Gift Tax Savings
• Maintain Control
• Teach Financial Responsibility to Children
• Benefit Charities
• You or Your Children Can Receive a Salary From the Foundation
• You Can Combine With a Wealth Replacement Insurance Trust to Replace the Donated Funds

Chapter 28. Generation Skipping Exemption Trust

      In some cases, children have received or will receive more than enough wealth for their lifetime, and by leaving them additional property you'll just be increasing the Estate Tax they will pay. You may also wish to leave part of your estate directly to your grandchildren, as well as provide for future generations. The tax law allows each spouse to leave your Lifetime Estate Tax Exemption (2011 = $5,000,000) directly to their grandchildren and to subsequent generations without incurring a second Estate Tax at your children's generation.

      The Generation Skipping Exemption Trust can be used to accomplish this. This is the Trust that is commonly used to avoid Estate Taxes on inherited assets that your children would otherwise be leaving to your grandchildren.

	Without GST Trust	With GST Trust
Investment Value	$1,000,000	$1,000,000
Estate Tax - Your Death	- 350,000	- 350,000
	$ 650,000	$ 650,000
Estate Tax - Your Child's Death	- 225,000	-0-
Net To Grandchildren	$ 425,000	$ 650,000

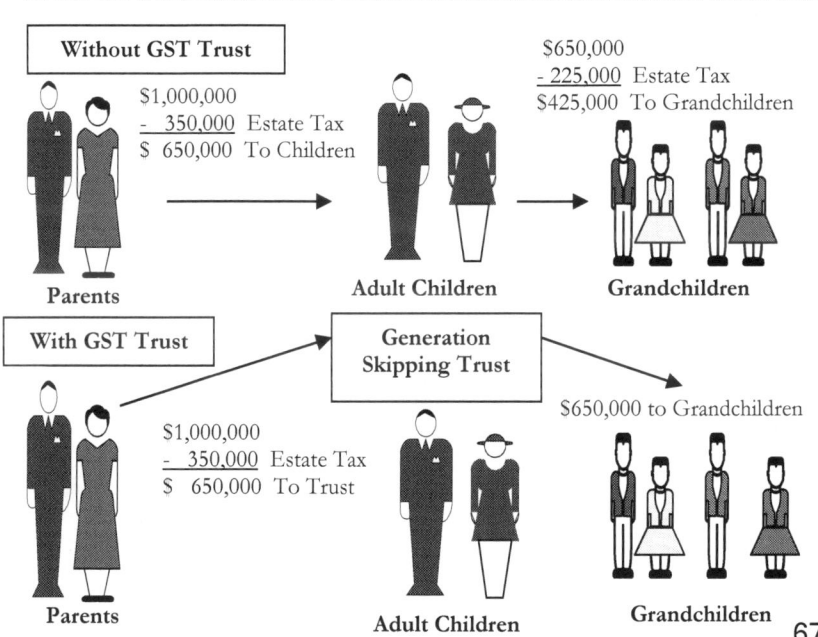

Without GST Trust

$1,000,000
- 350,000 Estate Tax
$ 650,000 To Children

$650,000
- 225,000 Estate Tax
$425,000 To Grandchildren

Parents

Adult Children

Grandchildren

With GST Trust

Generation Skipping Trust

$1,000,000
- 350,000 Estate Tax
$ 650,000 To Trust

$650,000 to Grandchildren

Parents

Adult Children

Grandchildren

Chapter 29. Illustrations

Impact on Total Estate Tax.

By implementing a gifting program, your Federal Estate Taxes can be substantially reduced.   The following example provides an illustration using some of the techniques discussed earlier.

Facts	Assumptions
• Family-owned business • Stock Value Today = $10M • 10% Growth each year for 10 Years • Stock Value 2021 = $25M • Married Couple Need $5 M of Life Exemption for other assets at death. • Transaction in 2011 • Death in 2021 • 2011 Estate/Gift Tax System • "S" Corporation	1. 35% Estate Tax Rate 2. Interest Rate GRAT = 3.0% IDGT = 2.0% 3. Calc's Roughed & Simplified for Illustration 4. Ignored Income Tax Effect **Other Considerations** GRAT – Owner must survive GRAT Life

Example: Transfer To Children - - Results At Death

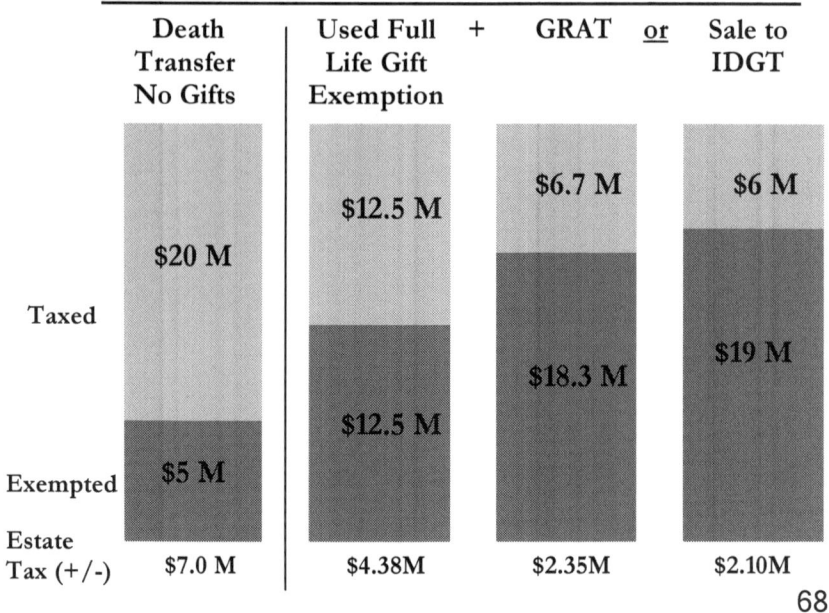

	Death Transfer No Gifts	Used Full + Life Gift Exemption	GRAT or	Sale to IDGT
Taxed	$20 M	$12.5 M	$6.7 M	$6 M
Exempted	$5 M	$12.5 M	$18.3 M	$19 M
Estate Tax (+/-)	$7.0 M	$4.38M	$2.35M	$2.10M

Estate Planning For Business Owners

Estate Planning For Business Owners

Have you established your family's and your Company's financial security if the unexpected happens to you? Depending on your personal situation, you may have several financial and personal goals and objectives.

These may include ongoing financial support for your spouse and family, education funding for your children and grandchildren, charitable funding for your favorite charities, and helping to assure that your assets are transferred to your family members upon your death as quickly and simply as possible.

You may also have personal financial objectives which involve protection of your assets against unwarranted and unexpected, but potential future creditor claims. These may be either from business operation exposures, personal accidents, personal injury or other casualties and contingencies.

In addition, you may want to assure that your estate, including your business interests, is arranged in a fashion to minimize potential death taxes.

Lastly, you may want to address certain objectives for determining what is needed for running your business if something happens to you before your planned exit.

When you are also a business owner, these personal and financial objectives need to be considered in the context of the added impact which your company has on your ability to achieve them.

For Bob and Betty, this part of our discussion especially piqued their interest. Their previous Estate Planning Attorney had not tailored the standard Estate Planning needs to the special needs which exist for business owners.

This step addresses these needs and opportunities.

Chapter 30. Business Owner Transition Growth Plan

Studies have demonstrated that most businesses do not survive the transition from the first generation to the second generation. Few make it to the third generation. Often the reason is because the owners are so busy just operating the business that they fail to take the time to implement a Business Owner Transition Growth Plan (also known as a Succession Plan or Exit Plan).

A Business Owner Transition Growth Plan is much like a Business Strategic Plan. However, instead of detailing how the business plans to operate to generate a profit, the Business Owner Transition Growth Plan details the means by which an owner or owners will provide for keeping the business intact, successful and growing during their remaining tenure as well as upon the succession of the business to new family members or new owners upon the owner's retirement, disability or death.

In addition to the Plan itself, a successful Business Owner Transition Growth Plan requires careful communication between owners and key employees, as well as the execution of certain additional documents.

The objectives business owners need to consider and the actions to address them are:

12 Objectives			12 Actions
Decide			
1.	What I Want	→ 1.	Owner Blueprint
2.	What I've Got	→ 2.	Company Valuation
Protect			
3.	My Family	→ 3.	Business Owner Estate Plan
4.	My Business	→ 4.	Asset Protection Program
5.	My Ownership	→ 5.	Buy-Sell Agreement
Grow			
6.	My Investments	→ 6.	Personal Wealth Plan
7.	My Business	→ 7.	Business Model Innovation Program
Prepare			
8.	My Management	→ 8.	Leadership Development Program
9.	My Company	→ 9.	Company Constitution
10.	My Tax Savings Plan	→ 10.	Coordinated Tax Plan
Exit			
11.	Via Inside Route	→ 11.	Inside Route Exit Plan
12.	Via Outside Route	→ 12.	Outside Route Exit Plan

This Guide addresses only the Business Owner Estate Plan. I have authored a separate book which details the specific actions which business owners need to take. The book is titled "The Next Move For Business Owners – The Transition, Growth and Exit Planning Strategies You Need To Know". This is available at www.OwnersNextMove.com.

BUSINESS OWNER TRANSITION GROWTH PLAN

Some Common Components:

- Shareholder Agreement
- Salary Continuation Plan
- Stock Redemption Plan
- Voting Trust
- Buy-Sell Agreement

- Deferred Compensation Agreement
- Split Dollar Insurance
- Key Man Insurance
- Disability Plan
- Subchapter "S" Protection Agreement

BENEFITS

- Minimize Loss of the Family Business From Family or Shareholder Disputes
- Protects Dad and Mom and Family upon a Death or Disability
- Transition Family Business to Next Generation or to New Owners

Chapter 31. Business Owner Estate Plan Provisions

While the Estate Planning needs of a business owner include the same issues as non-business owners, your business ownership brings into play a series of additional Estate Planning issues and options to be addressed.

As the owner of a business, you will often have Estate Planning needs which extend beyond the typical Estate Plan. This may be due to certain financial or business needs of the business or because of particular family issues which are already present or may arise upon your death or disability. Many of these matters can be covered with a Living Trust by using a Business Owner Living Trust.

$$\begin{array}{ccccc} \textbf{Basic} & & \textbf{Business} & & \textbf{Business} \\ \textbf{Estate} & + & \textbf{Owner} & = & \textbf{Owner} \\ \textbf{Plan} & & \textbf{Living} & & \textbf{Estate} \\ & & \textbf{Trust} & & \textbf{Plan} \end{array}$$

In order to help address the business owner's specific Estate Planning issues, you may want to consider the use of the following tools.

- **Specific Bequest to Business-Active Children.** If you have one or more children who are active in the business and one or more children who are not, you need to consider whether you want to make a specific bequest of your business ownership interest to the active children in you Business Owner Living Trust, so that they have ownership control as well as the valuation benefit on account of their decision to be active in your business.

- **Non-Active Children Equalization.** When the business ownership has been specifically allocated in your estate to one or more children active in the business, an equalizing share can be allocated to non-active children through a specific bequest of other financial assets in your Business Owner Living Trust. If your estate does not have sufficient other financial assets to fully equalize the shares, then at least two other options exist. This can include a split off of non-operating business assets into a separate leasing or licensing entity

73

which can be allocated to the non-active children. This would still leave the business operating assets intact in the business entity to be owned by the active children. As an alternative, life insurance can be obtained which would help fund the equalization to the non-active children.

- **Family Business Representative.** Typically an Estate Plan will appoint a personal representative (executor) and a successor trustee to handle financial and business decisions for your estate. In those situations where that representative or trustee is not well-equipped to make business decisions impacting your ongoing business, a family business representative can be appointed in your Estate Plan to make business decisions relating to management of the business. You have at least two ways this can be done. First, this representative can be given authority in your Business Owner Living Trust to override your regular trustee's authority. Second, the representative can be viewed as essentially an advisor, whose decisions are subject to the overriding decision-making authority of your regular successor trustee.

- **Business Sale Instructions.** As part of your Transition Growth Plan, if you have not completed your exit from your business at the time of your death or disability, but believe that the best alternative for the family is that the business be sold, then your Transition Growth Plan and/or Business Owner Living Trust should contain sufficient details to provide instructions on how and to whom your business can best be sold or transferred should you die or become disabled before you complete your exit.

- **Successor CEO.** Your Transition Growth Plan and/or Business Owner Living Trust can also designate your recommended successor CEO for the business. This is particularly important if at least two children may each claim that you intended to appoint them to run the company.

- **Contingency Plan Notifications.** Your Transition Growth Plan and/or Business Owner Living Trust should also contain contingency plan notifications to your family and to your Board of Directors which detail the immediate steps to be taken upon your death or disability.

- **"Sweat" Equity Allocation.** You may decide that your estate is not to be divided exactly equally between your children due to a difference between the role which your children have played in the success or operation of your business. Your Business Owner Living Trust can include an allocation with regard to your business assets which recognizes the "sweat equity" contribution of those children who have been active in the business but who have been under-compensated based on their contribution to the success of the business.

- **Dispute Resolution.** If you have more than one child, it is possible your estate will encounter a dispute once you are no longer present. Your Business Owner Living Trust can include a dispute resolution provision which prevents a dissatisfied child from disrupting business operations. A dispute resolution provision can range from the appointment of a mediator to help resolve disputes, to instead including a provision which disinherits a child who challenges your Estate Plan.

- **Financial Resource Reserve.** If your business needs your ongoing financial support in order to thrive, then your Business Owner Living Trust can designate that a reserve portion of your estate be held as a financial resource to help support the business and/or its credit needs.

- **Family Council.** Your Business Owner Living Trust can designate a Family Council to be established to enable your spouse and adult children to be apprised of ongoing business operations and to discuss resolution of business matters impacting the family. Depending on the make up of your family and your use of a board of directors, in lieu of a Family Council, you can consider having your children serve on your Board of Directors as either voting or non-voting board members, as an additional way to keep the family members apprised of the ongoing challenges associated with the business.

- **Business Key Person Life Insurance.** This enables the business to receive cash proceeds to help overcome the loss of key personnel.

- **Business Buy-Out Life Insurance.** This enables the company to receive cash proceeds to help fund the buy-out upon the death of an owner and is addressed as part of a Buy-Sell Agreement.

Business Owner Estate Plan Provisions

☑ Special Bequest to Business-Active Children

☑ Non-Active Children Equalization

☑ Family Business Representative

☑ Business Sale Instructions

☑ Successor CEO

☑ Contingency Plan Notifications

☑ "Sweat" Equity Allocation

☑ Dispute Resolution

☑ Financial Resource Reserve

☑ Family Council

☑ Business Key Person Life Insurance

☑ Business Buy-Out Life Insurance

☑ Transition, Succession & Exit Plan Matters

To Do List

√ _____

√ _____

√ _____

√ _____

√ _____

Estate Planning Uses of Insurance

Estate Planning Uses of Insurance

Bob and Betty had purchased some term life insurance policies when the children were younger. They realized that the death of either of them would have resulted in an obvious need to have a financial resource to replace that income to support their family. What they had not really addressed was the large array of insurance products and features which could serve their families personally, but could also address the needs of their business continuity.

Often when I bring up the topic of insurance coverage, I am first met with a series of groans and requests to please talk about anything else. I suppose this is largely due to misconceptions about insurance, along with the desire to avoid considering the circumstances that result in insurance proceeds being paid -- death, disability, accident, illness, etc. My suggestion is this -- get over it.

Insurance is a tremendous product that, when properly purchased and utilized has the ability to protect your savings, create wealth, replace wealth, support you and your loved ones and/or pay for taxes and expenses that you'd rather not have to pay for or may be unable to pay for. Without proper insurance coverages, you are taking on needless and irresponsible risks for yourself and your family.

Insurance is one of the best tools for accomplishing the main objective in Estate Planning, and the theme of this Guide, that is, providing savings, protection, opportunities and peace-of-mind to families.

Some of the uses of the various types of insurance in Estate Planning include the following:

Personal	Business
• Expense Coverage	• Key Employee Loss Coverage
• Income Replacement	• Buy-Sell Agreement Funding
• Mortgage Payoff	• Key Employee Benefit Funding
• Investment Stability and Growth	• Deferred Compensation Funding
• Wealth Creation	• Salary Continuation Funding
• Disability Coverage	• Retirement Plan Funding
• Long Term Care Coverage	• Business Interruption Coverage
• Estate Equalization	• Business Owner Transitions
• Education Expense Coverage	
• Death Tax Payment	

This part of the Guide will briefly consider some of the uses of insurance in Estate Planning. It is by no means exhaustive. Instead, it only scratches the surface of the benefits available.

Lastly, don't enter in without proper guidance. The assistance of a competent and professional insurance adviser is invaluable.

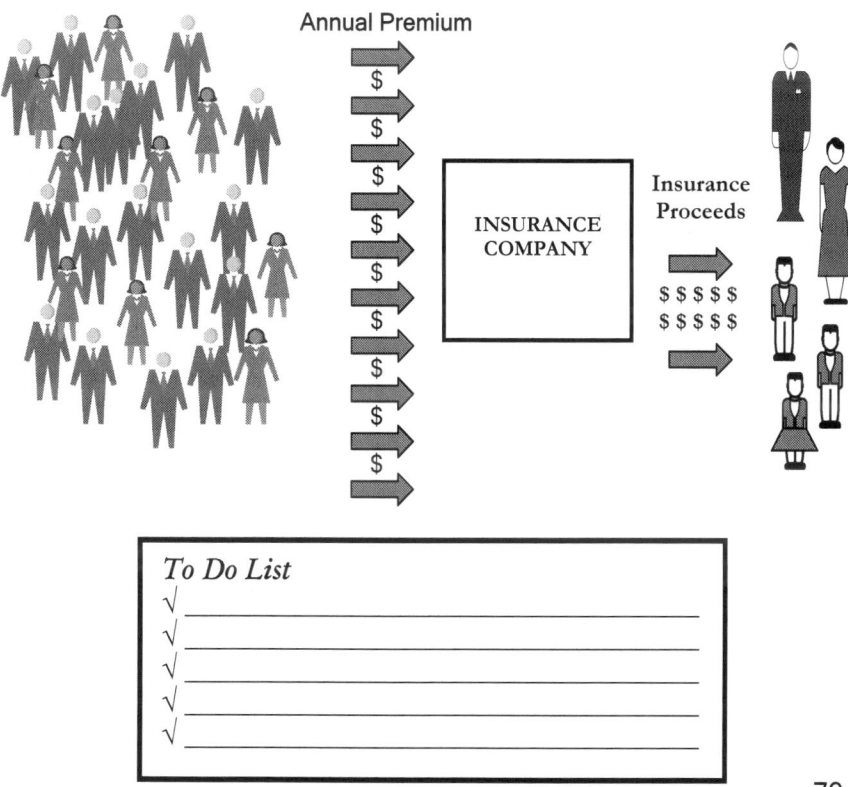

Chapter 32. Income Replacement Life Insurance

One of the most obvious and most common purposes of owning Life Insurance is to provide immediate and substantial funds to provide income to the surviving spouse and children if the income provider should die.

This is true for families where either one or both spouses are employed. If the sole income provider dies, the need for funds to replace the lost income is obvious. It is generally difficult for a surviving stay-at-home spouse to return to the workplace at an income level equal to that of the deceased spouse. While in a two income family, the loss of one income provider means a substantial reduction in family income.

For a family that depends on a paycheck (that is, most families), the question is not whether income replacement life insurance is needed. The questions are how much is needed and what type of insurance should be owned.

The most common types of insurance are term insurance, whole life insurance, variable life insurance and universal life insurance. Term insurance typically involves less annual premium cash outlay with no return until death and no build up of cash value. Whole life, variable and universal insurance typically involves a higher annual premium cash outlay, with the opportunity to accumulate tax free or tax deferred investment savings in a policy that builds a cash value that can be accessed before death or if you cancel the policy.

The question of how much depends on the amount of income you need to replace and how long you need to replace it for. A simple rule of thumb is you should carry life insurance at least equal to 15 to 20 times your annual after tax take home pay. This needs to be adjusted based on additional funding needed for child education expenses and other special needs.

Your financial planner, investment adviser, accountant and/or life insurance adviser can provide a more detailed analysis of the type and amount of life insurance best for you.

If you've decided you don't want your Estate to go immediately upon your death into the hands of your children, then it's important to name your Living Trust as the beneficiary of your life insurance. This enables the proceeds to be used for your surviving spouse and then be held for and/or distributed to your children at the times designated in your Trust.

Life insurance proceeds are not normally taxed for income tax purposes. However, if your Estate exceeds $5,000,000 ($10,000,000 if married) then your life insurance is generally subject to Estate Taxes -- unless you use a Life Insurance Trust as the owner and beneficiary of your life insurance.

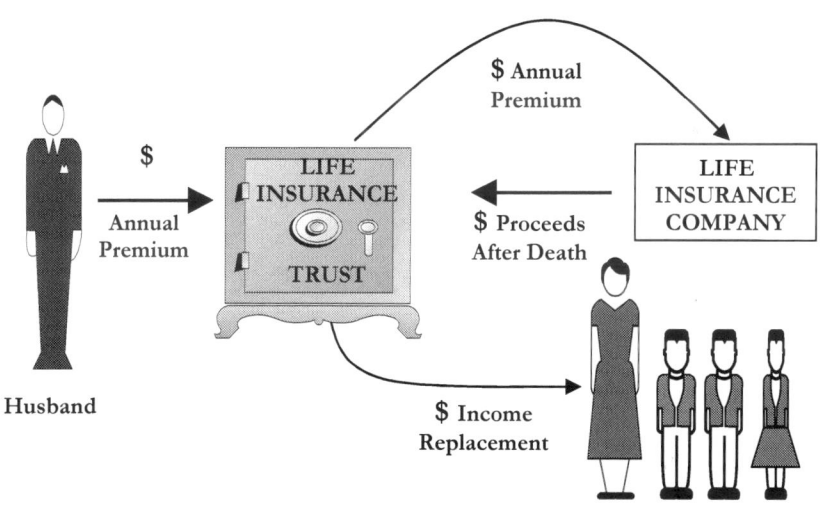

To Do List
√ _____
√ _____
√ _____
√ _____
√ _____

Chapter 33. Estate Tax Payment Life Insurance

If your Estate exceeds your Lifetime Estate Tax Exemption ($5,000,000 each. $10,000,000 if married), then after the death of both spouses, your family will need to pay Estate Taxes out of your Estate. For the sake of estimating, the Estate Tax will be about 35% of the value of your Estate in excess of the above amount.

Two principal reasons exist for owning life insurance with the specific purposes of paying Estate Taxes.

First, if you'd like your heirs to receive a certain amount, and Estate Taxes would reduce your net Estate below that amount even after you've taken the Estate Tax reduction steps available to you, then you may want to invest in Life Insurance. This can be used to pay Estate Taxes.

Second, if you don't have enough liquid assets (cash, stocks, bonds, mutual funds) to pay the Estate Taxes and own assets that aren't easily converted to cash (or that can be converted only at fire sale reduced prices) or assets you don't want sold (such as a family business), then you may want to invest in Life Insurance to cover the Estate Taxes.

If you are in either of these situations, then you don't want to add to the total Estate Tax due by having the Life Insurance be subject to Estate Taxes. This is typically best handled by having a Life Insurance Trust own and be the beneficiary of the Life Insurance.

If you are married, and since Estate Tax is not due until after the death of both spouses, you generally should use Joint Life - Life Insurance (also known as Second-To-Die or Survivor Life Insurance) to pay the Estate Taxes. This insurance pays out only after both spouses have died, that is, at the time the funds are actually needed. Because the insurance is based on the life expectancy of two persons (instead of just one), the premium is generally much less than a Single Life - Life Insurance policy.

Your Financial Planner, Investment Adviser, Accountant and/or Life Insurance Adviser can provide a more detailed analysis of the type and amount of life insurance best for you.

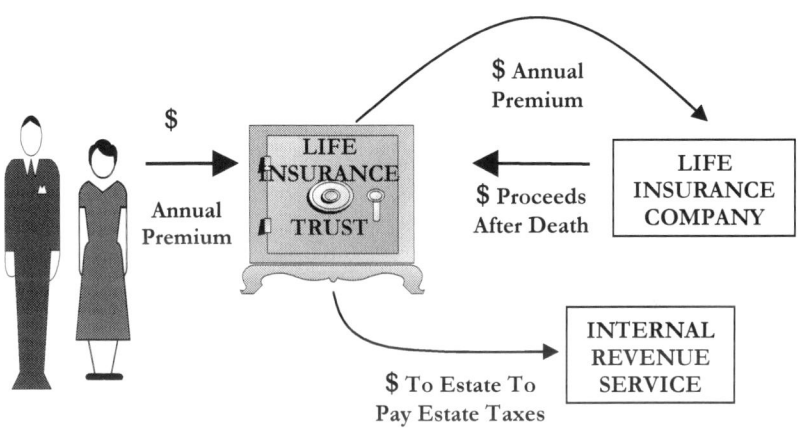

To Do List

√ _____

√ _____

√ _____

√ _____

√ _____

Chapter 34. Asset Protection Umbrella Insurance

Homeowner and automobile insurance coverage typically only cover $300,000 to $500,000 of maximum accident liability. However, actual damages in a bad accident could be assessed against you far in excess of this.

One of the best ways to help provide asset protection and preserve your savings to cover the risk of such accidents is to add Umbrella Insurance coverage. This insurance sits on top of your homeowners and automobile insurance coverage and provides you with protection against a vast array of risks.

This insurance can typically be purchased in increments of $1 million up to $5 million. The annual premium cost is only a few hundred dollars per million dollars over coverage.

It's a small investment to make to help protect your life savings from being depleted by a major liability.

Your Living Trust can be named as an additional insured under such policies.

BENEFITS

- Protects You Against Liability for Major Accidents.
- Relatively Inexpensive.

To Do List
√ _____
√ _____
√ _____
√ _____
√ _____

Chapter 35. Long-Term Care Insurance

Long Term Care Insurance has become a popular and affordable way to pay for the prospect of long term care costs. Neither Medicare nor your private health insurance will pay these costs. Government provided Medicaid will pay these costs, however, this program only applies if your net worth is minimal.

This means these costs are paid either by your savings or Long Term Care Insurance.

Over the past few decades the insurance industry has developed some very good long term care insurance products. The insurance industry is experiencing some issues with some of these products. This remains, however, an alternative that should be considered as part of your overall Estate Planning.

Your Living Trust can be designated as the recipient of your Long Term Care Insurance so that these funds are properly used if you are disabled.

In-home senior care services provide a very strong alternative to enable parents and grandparents to remain in their homes to receive the care and services they deserve while at the same time providing another effective way to manage the costs of care.

ODDS: Almost 1 of 2 Americans Over Age 65 Will Spend Part Of Their Life In A Nursing Home
(Health Magazine)
Average Annual Nursing Home Cost: $83,585
Average Annual Assisted Living Cost: $39,516
(2010 Market Survey of Long-Term Care Costs)

BENEFITS

• **Long Term Care Insurance** - Probably the Best Way to Pay for Long Term Care - Because:

– Medicare Won't Pay For It
– Medicaid Won't Apply Unless You Spend Most of Your Assets First

Estate Planning For Vacation Home Owners

Chapter 36 - Vacation Home Succession Plan

Estate Planning For Vacation Home Owners

For Bob and Betty, their lake cabin in Minnesota had been the ideal family retreat. Their three children, Jack, Joe and Jane, had learned to fish and water ski during their summer vacations and how to snow ski during their winter breaks. Their cabin had also been ideal for weekend get-a-ways, with the family also frequently hosting their childrens' friends and making over three decades of memories.

The cabin had become a second home for the family. And now, with Jack having children of his own, it was becoming a memory maker for Bob and Betty's grandchildren as well.

However, Bob and Betty's enjoyment of the family retreat was also the source of some worry. While they hoped their family would continue to always get along, they weren't so naïve to expect that would be the case. The last thing they wanted was for the cabin to become the source of disputes and heartaches.

Their previous Estate Planning Attorney had simply placed their vacation home into their Living Trust, to be distributed to the children equally after Bob and Betty passed away. While one of the reasons Bob and Betty had come to meet with me was to discuss their succession planning for their family business, we also decided to discuss their vacation home succession planning. They had specific questions they wanted to address about the future of the cabin after their deaths:

- What would happen to the cabin if one of the children died?
- What would happen if one of the children got divorced?
- What would happen if one of the children couldn't afford (or didn't want to pay) their share of expenses (or had future creditor problems)?
- What would happen if one of the children insisted on selling their share?

- What would happen if the children disagreed about how the cabin would be operated and maintained?
- How could the cabin's use be scheduled to avoid disputes?
- How could the cabin be preserved so it could be passed down to Bob and Betty's grandchildren after their children's deaths?
- How could this be accomplished in a tax efficient manner?

Bob and Betty presented the classic situation for Vacation Home Succession Planning. Vacation Home Succession Planning (also known as Cottage Succession Planning) refers to the legal and financial strategies used to help keep the family vacation home peacefully and effectively in the family for successive generations. These strategies can be used whether your vacation home is a million dollar second home overlooking the ocean or a small log cabin in the woods.

This form of advanced Estate Planning comes into play whenever a family has a cabin, beach house, cottage, lake home, camp, farmhouse, chalet, ski condo, hunting lodge, winter home, summer home, second home or other vacation home which they want to pass on to their heirs to keep in the family for future use and enjoyment. The use of a regular Estate Plan, even with a Living Trust, is not adequate. The questions which Bob and Betty had, along with others, are each addressed in a Vacation Home Succession Plan.

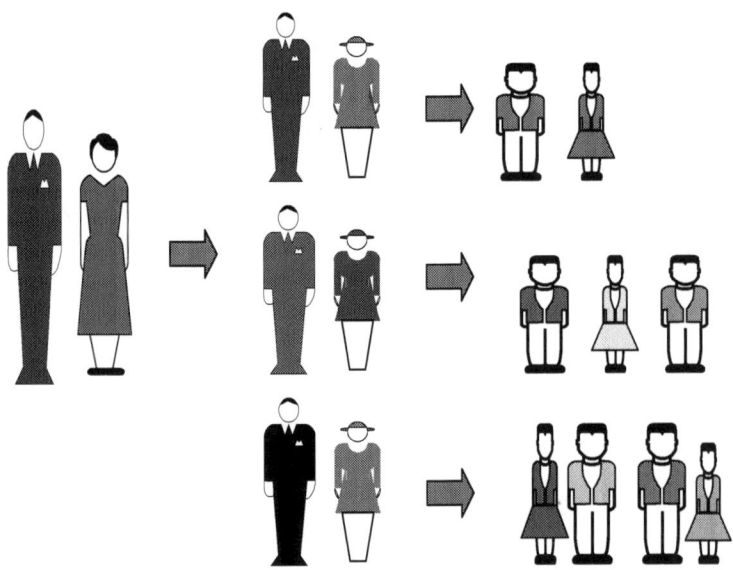

Chapter 36. Vacation Home Succession Plan

A Vacation Home Succession Plan is an Estate Planning strategy which can help parents and grandparents to ensure that their vacation home can successfully be passed on and maintained within the family by succeeding generations.

A Vacation Home Succession Plan typically includes the following:

- Transfer of the vacation home to a special purpose limited liability company ("LLC").
- Creation of an LLC Operating Agreement with special features to address the decision-making, scheduling and expenses of the vacation home and divorce and liability protection, as well as guidelines for future purchase and sale of ownership interests by one or more family members.
- A Dynasty Trust may be added in certain cases to hold the LLC shares. The family (children, grandchildren, great grandchildren, etc.) would be named as beneficiaries of the Trust. They would be entitled to use the vacation home but would not have any direct ownership of the LLC or the vacation home.
- A funding mechanism, such as a Vacation Home Endowment Fund, funded by either a share of the parents' estate, a life insurance policy, or a dedicated investment fund established by the parents (to be held in either the LLC or the Dynasty Trust).
- Investment management and banking guidelines for managing the Vacation Home Endowment Fund.

The LLC needs to be coordinated with the parents' Living Trust and Financial Power of Attorney.

Used for avoiding this:

Used for achieving this:

And this:

And this:

Estate Planning Mistakes

Chapter 37 - Avoiding 30 Estate Planning
Mistakes

Estate Planning Mistakes

Bob and Betty had seen too many friends who had suffered the consequences of making avoidable Estate Planning mistakes. They were not interested in suffering the same fate. So our discussion also addressed the steps needed to avoid common pitfalls.

I have found that there are 30 common Estate Planning mistakes often made by parents and grandparents. These are described below.

A properly prepared Estate Plan can be designed to overcome these. These take some time and effort to address with your Estate Planning Attorney and other advisors.

I have grouped these into the following 14 situations:

- If You Own Any Property
- If You Are Married
- If You Have Children
- If You Want to Keep Control Upon Your Disability
- If You Own Life Insurance
- If You Own Investments
- If You Own a Business, Profession or Farm
- If You Want to Avoid Probate Court
- If Your Estate Exceeds The Lifetime Estate Tax Exemption
- If You Have a Retirement Plan
- If You Want Family Gifts to Also Save Taxes
- If You Want to Keep Some Control Over Gifts
- If You Want to Give to Charity
- General Mistakes and Misperceptions

The following chapter details these 30 common Estate Planning mistakes and offers suggestions for avoiding them.

Chapter 37. Avoiding 30 Estate Planning Mistakes

If You Own Any Property
1. Not having a Will or Living Trust.
    *   Without a Will or funded Living Trust the State Statutes specify who receives your separate property.

If You Are Married
2. Leaving your Estate to your spouse without protecting your spouse from unforeseen accident litigation risks.
    *   A Living Trust can help address this.

If You Have Children
3. Having a Will or Trust that leaves your property directly to minors, grandchildren or young adult children who are not yet financially responsible.
    *   A Living Trust enables child and grandchild inheritance to be protected in trust until designated time or age.

4. Leaving no instructions for raising your children if you die or are disabled.
    *   An Estate Planning Letter can address this.

5. Not naming your hand-picked guardian for minor children.
    *   Your Will can accomplish this.

If You Want to Keep Control Upon Your Disability
6. Letting the Courts control your financial and health care matters if you become disabled.
    *   A Financial Power of Attorney and Health Care Power of Attorney can avoid this.

If You Own Life Insurance
7. Not having the right amount and types of insurance to cover your and your family's living expenses and taxes after your death.
    *   A Life Insurance Needs Plan can help determine the Life Insurance needed.

8. Owning your life insurance directly, if your Estate exceeds the Lifetime Estate Tax Exemption.
    *   A Life Insurance Exemption Trust can be used to avoid the approximate 35% Estate Tax on life insurance.

If You Own Investments
9. Having no direction to continue your present investment management upon your disability or death.
    *   A Living Trust can address this.

10. Owning property in Joint Tenancy with children.
    *   This can subject parents to their childrens' creditors.

If You Own a Business, Profession or Farm
11. Not having a written agreement covering buy-out and business succession for your business or profession.
    *   This can be addressed with a Buy-Sell Agreement or Shareholder Agreement.

12. Not being prepared to sell or transfer your company or for the expected or unexpected retirement, death or disability of company owners.
    *   This can be addressed with a Transition Growth Plan (www.OwnersNextMove.com).

If You Want to Avoid Probate Court
13. Holding title to your separate property directly in your name.
    *   Property re-titled to your Living Trust before death avoids Probate Court.

If Your Estate Exceeds The Lifetime Estate Tax Exemption
14. Forfeiting one of your Lifetime Estate Tax Exemptions by using a Simple Will or Joint Tenancy with your spouse.
    *   A Simple Will and Joint Tenancy fail to set aside property to obtain the exemption. Relying on exemption portability is not sufficient since it doesn't cover valuation growth after the first death.

15. Having a Will or Trust that doesn't automatically allow for change to the Estate Tax exemption.
    *   Your Estate Plan can be drafted to allow for this.

16. Failing to properly balance property ownership between spouses.

- Balancing Spouse Ownership helps assure each spouse has sufficient property to fully use the full benefit of both Lifetime Estate Tax Exemptions.

17. Having the wrong type, or an improperly drafted, marital deduction in a Will or Trust that doesn't comply with IRS requirements (resulting in Estate Tax on the death of the first spouse) or doesn't protect your children.
    - An outright marital deduction must comply with IRS Rev. Proc. 64-19. A life estate (QTIP) marital deduction must comply with Tax Code 2056.

If You Have a Retirement Plan

18. Incorrect Retirement Plan Distribution Elections and Beneficiary Designations.
    - Proper Beneficiary Designations to a spouse and/or Living Trust can minimize taxes, help avoid Probate, and help preserve funds for the family. Proper Distribution Elections upon retirement can minimize income taxes.

19. Not considering the permitted stretch-out options to extend the compounded, tax deferred benefits of your retirement plans.
    - Use of a Stretch-Out IRA in appropriate circumstances can extend the retirement savings tax deferral.

20. Using your retirement savings instead of considering the right long-term care insurance products to cover your expenses of long-term or nursing home care.
    - Long-Term Care Insurance can protect your retirement savings.

If You Want Family Gifts to Also Save Taxes

21. Failing to use available Estate Tax reduction techniques.
    - Property gifted during your life to children and grandchildren is not subject to your Estate Tax. Using your Annual Exemption Gifts ($13,000) and/or your Lifetime Gift Tax Exemption can reduce Estate Taxes.
    - Investments gifted through a Family Limited Partnership or Limited Liability Company can be value-discounted to increase the tax benefit of your Exemption Gifts.

22. Naming yourself as custodian under the UTMA for gifts to your children or grandchildren if your Estate exceeds the Lifetime Estate Tax Exemption.

- This would result in the gifts still being taxed in your Estate for Estate Tax purposes.

If You Want to Keep Some Control Over Gifts

23. Making substantial lifetime gifts directly to minors, grandchildren or your adult children who are not yet financially responsible.
    - Use of a Family Limited Partnership or Limited Liability Company can provide certain controls and protection by holding gifts for children and grandchildren.

If You Want to Give to Charity

24. Failing to arrange to complete your lifetime charitable giving if you die prematurely.
    - A Will or Living Trust can be used to make bequests to charities effective upon your death. A Family Private Foundation or Charitable Remainder Trust can also be used to establish a charitable giving program.

General Mistakes and Misperceptions

25. Thinking that Estate Planning only deals with what happens when you die.
    - Estate Planning also protects assets while you're alive, healthy or disabled.

26. Thinking that Estate Planning is only for the wealthy.
    - Estate Planning deals with issues affecting families regardless of the size of their Estate.

27. Focusing first on avoiding Estate Taxes and Probate rather than first on what it takes to maintain control and to protect yourself and your family upon retirement, disability, accident or death.
    - All of these are important, but the primary objective is to maintain control by parents of their Estate and to protect the family.

28. Having an Estate Plan that uses short term thinking and doesn't properly provide for contingencies.
    - An Estate Plan needs to be drafted to anticipate life and asset changes – to the extent reasonably feasible.

29. Waiting until you believe you have everything exactly ready before doing your Estate Plan and never getting it done.
    - Estate Planning is less complicated than most people think.

30. Failing to update your Estate Plan through periodic check-ups or upon significant life or asset changes.
    • Laws, family, life and finances change. Your Estate Plan should be periodically reviewed to address these changes.

```
┌─────────────────────────────────────────────┐
│  To Do List                                   │
│  √ _____   │
│  √ _____   │
│  √ _____   │
│  √ _____   │
│  √ _____   │
└─────────────────────────────────────────────┘
```

What's Your Next Move?

Chapter 38 -   Are You Prepared?

What's Your Next Move?

We all go through life in a constant state of either being ready or not for the events and circumstances which we will face. This is equally true for our Estate Planning.

The fact is we really don't know when we might become disabled, when we might face an unexpected financial adversity, or when we will exit this life. The reality is that even the best laid plans can change quickly (or at least more quickly than we anticipated), due to unforeseen business, financial, personal, health and family changes in circumstances.

The Boy Scout motto is "be prepared". It is good advice, and it is particularly applicable in Estate Planning.

Just as you would not take a trip or undertake some new venture without adequate preparation, you wouldn't want to venture into your foreseeable or unforeseeable future without adequate preparation.

So. Where do you stand? How ready are you for the expected or the unexpected? Bob and Betty are now ready. Are you?

Below is an Estate Plan Fitness Test which we've designed to help you to answer that question. At the end of this test you should have a better idea of the answers to the following two fundamental questions:

Fundamental Questions.

I intend to address the following questions:

☐ What will be the probable, almost certain, future outcome of my present course, if left unchanged?

☐ What's missing, the presence of which would make a substantial difference in producing a better outcome?

Estate Plan Fitness Test

This Test is part of the "History and Physical" we utilize in the Estate Planning process. Read the questions carefully. Be honest with yourself. If you don't know an answer for sure, it should be answered "No". A few questions might be "not applicable" to you. Leave those blank.

		YES	NO
Decide What I Want.			
1.	Do I know for sure who I want to transfer my Estate to and when I want them to receive it outright after my death?	☐	☐
2.	Do I know for sure who I want to handle my financial and health care matters if I am unable to do so?	☐	☐
3.	Do I know in which State I want to reside after I retire?	☐	☐
4.	Do I know for sure how much cash-in-pocket I need or want upon my retirement (or my family needs after my death) to achieve financial independence?	☐	☐
Decide What I've Got.		**YES**	**NO**
5.	Do I know the net value of my property?	☐	☐
6.	Do I know how much life, disability and long-term care insurance I have or need?	☐	☐
7.	Do I have a recent, written Personal Financial Statement?	☐	☐
Protect My Family.		**YES**	**NO**
8.	Have I executed a durable financial power of attorney which is a "present power" which designates a capable person (and capable successors) to handle my financial affairs upon my disability?	☐	☐
9.	Have I executed a durable health care power of attorney which designates a capable individual (and capable successors) to handle my medical affairs upon my disability and which is HIPAA compliant.	☐	☐

10. Have I executed a health care directive (living will) which specifies proper guidelines for utilizing or maintaining health care procedures in extraordinary circumstances? ☐ ☐

11. Have I executed a pour-over will to designate a capable personal representative (executor) and capable successors to handle my estate (including business matters) and guardian for any minor children upon my death? ☐ ☐

12. Have I executed a living trust which protects my spouse and which protects my children and grandchildren until designated ages? ☐ ☐

13. Have I re-titled my assets into my living trust (including my business assets) in order to avoid probate court intervention with regard to my estate and my business? ☐ ☐

14. Have I appointed capable successor trustees to my living trust who understand my financial and business operations? ☐ ☐

15. Have I addressed my charitable giving objectives, in particular from a tax favored perspective? ☐ ☐

16. Have I addressed my education funding objectives? ☐ ☐

17. Have I implemented the applicable personal Asset Protection Plan tools, given an assessment of my personal exposure to business and personal contingent liability risks? ☐ ☐

18. Have I addressed specific bequests and equalization to and amongst children who are active or inactive in any business I own? ☐ ☐

19. Have I designated in my Estate Plan how my personal representative (executor), family business representative or trustee is to manage or sell my assets or my business upon my death or disability? ☐ ☐

20. Have I included in my Estate Plan a dispute resolution provision which prevents a dissatisfied child from disrupting my financial or business operations? ☐ ☐

21. Have I recently evaluated my personal life and disability insurance needs and implemented the insurance coverage appropriate to addressing my ☐ ☐

financial gap, needs and objectives?

22. Have I established a sufficient retirement plan or a funded salary continuation plan or agreement to provide ongoing support to my spouse and family upon my death or disability? ☐ ☐

23. Do I have a professionally prepared Wealth Plan? ☐ ☐

Handle My Business Ownership.   YES   NO

24. Will my spouse or family be able to receive cash for the full value of my business upon my death or disability? ☐ ☐

25. Do I have an exit plan letter to my family, with written instructions to my spouse and family for handling business matters upon my death or disability? ☐ ☐

26. Do I have pre-written guidelines for assisting my spouse, family and advisers in selling the company to a third party or insiders upon my death or disability? ☐ ☐

27. Do I have pre-written designation to my spouse, family and/or board of directors naming principal exit plan advisors to assist in advising family and my board of directors on the transition of business matters upon my death or disability? ☐ ☐

28. Have I established a Buy-Sell Agreement for my business which establishes must/may buy obligations on death, disability, employment termination, retirement, bankruptcy and divorce of all shareholders? ☐ ☐

29. Have I established a Buy-Sell Agreement which establishes the right type of stock pricing? ☐ ☐

30. Have I provided sufficient funding for the Buy-Sell obligations under our Buy-Sell agreement? ☐ ☐

31. Do I have a written Transition Growth Plan (also known as a Succession Plan or Exit Plan) for each business I own? ☐ ☐

Prepare My Tax Savings Plans.   YES   NO

32. Have I executed a living trust which properly establishes the appropriate marital deduction provisions and federal estate tax exemption utilization for both spouses? ☐ ☐

33. Have I implemented appropriate estate tax reduction tools, such as annual exemption gifting, ☐ ☐

family limited liability partnership (or LLC), lifetime exemption gifting, a gifting power of attorney and irrevocable life insurance trust, as applicable?

Overall.

	YES	NO
40. Do I believe I am as prepared and up-to-date as I should be for my Estate Planning?	☐	☐
TOTALS		

	Ready	Not Ready

Achieving Your Legacy

As parents of six children and grandparents of seven grandchildren (so far), my wife Ann and I, like all parents and grandparents, want to do everything we can to help assure their protection and well-being.

If you are like us, you don't have a lot of time to become experts in everything you need to get done. That is why I've tried in this short Guide to provide the essence of the actions which I believe all parents and grandparents need to be working on with their Financial Advisor and Estate Planning Attorney.

My hope is this Guide will help you to make your "next move" towards protecting your families.

As we began this Estate Planning Guide, we focused on your personal and financial objectives. This is exactly what I first focus on with each new Estate Planning client who is referred to me. If you keep the vision of those objectives in the forefront as you address your Estate Planning, your likelihood of being successful will be substantially increased and your happiness with this process will be more thoroughly realized.

That's why the final strategy in the Estate Planning process which I stress with both new and existing Estate Planning clients is to first look forward as you begin the process to the end result you're trying to achieve, visualize the legacy you want to leave, and then enjoy the peace-of-mind that a solid Estate Plan will provide for you and your family.

APPENDIX

Your Personal and Financial Objectives

What are your personal and financial objectives? ☐:

☐ To begin spending less time running my business by handing over certain operating duties to one or more key employees.

☐ To begin to travel more with my spouse and/or other family members, starting with a _____ week trip to _____ during 20___.

☐ To be able to travel more to visit my grandchildren at least _____ times per year.

☐ To be able to spend more time on my charitable activities.

☐ To assume that my spouse does not need to become entangled negotiating financial matters with my co-owners, employees or creditors upon my unexpected death or disability.

☐ To assure that I'm not leaving my spouse or family with a "Junk Drawer" of business and financial matters to try to untangle upon my unexpected death or disability.

☐ To work for another _____ years, and to develop one or more of my insiders (adult children or key employee(s)) to be my successor in the business.

☐ To leave my estate equally to my children.

☐ To leave my business to one or more of my adult children and equalize shares to my other children.

☐ To assure that my estate is not distributed too early to my young adult children, but instead is distributed over time as they reach designated ages.

☐ To assure that any portion of my estate left to one of my adult children who dies leaving surviving children, is held in trust for the protection of those grandchildren.

☐ To assure that if I die, my spouse has an investment net worth (cash-in-pocket) of at least $_____.

☐ To assure that if I am disabled, my spouse and I have an annual after tax net income of at least $_____.

☐ To be free of potential contingent liabilities and business debt guarantees by _____, 20___.

☐ To be free of personal debt by _____, 20___.

☐ To be able to leave a net worth of at least $_____ to my children upon my death.

- ☐ To be able to establish a $_____ charitable fund for my favorite charities.
- ☐ To utilize a portion of my business exit proceeds to invest in another business enterprise as either a passive or active owner.
- ☐ To help assure that my business will be carried on after my planned or unexpected exit to help provide ongoing financial security for other family members (e.g. siblings and adult children) and/or long time, loyal key employees.
- ☐ To help assure that my business continues after my planned or unexpected exit in order to help provide ongoing products and services to my loyal customers/clients/patients.
- ☐ To maximize the potential sale price and minimize the income tax hit for myself and my family upon the sale of my business.
- ☐ To assure that upon my unexpected death or disability, that my company has adequate funding to continue in my absence.
- ☐ To minimize estate taxes.
- ☐ To provide education funding for my children and/or grandchildren.
- ☐ To keep my business and personal assets out of probate.
- ☐ Other _____
  _____
- ☐ Other _____
  _____
- ☐ Other _____
  _____
- ☐ Other _____
  _____

What is the legacy you want to leave?: _____
_____
_____
_____

What are the next moves you are going to take to help achieve this?: _____
_____
_____
_____

INDEX

F

Family Business Representative · 74
Family Council · 75
Family Limited Partnership · 17, 57, 59, 94, 95
Federal Estate Tax · 10
Financial Resource Reserve · 75
Funded Living Trust · 23, 26, 27
Funeral Wishes · 37

G

Generation Skipping Exemption Trust · 53, 54, 67
Generation-Skipping tax · 55
Gift Protection Trust · 17
Gift Tax · 56
Government Estate Plan · 4, 6, 7
Grantor Retained Annuity Trust · 53, 63

I

Income Replacement · 78
Income Replacement Life Insurance · 77
Information Organizer · 37
Inside Route Exit Plan · 71
Insurance Coverage · 52
Intentionally Defective Grantor Trust · 64
Investment Protection · 51
Investment Stability and Growth · 78
Irrevocable Trust · 51

J

Joint Tenancy · 10, 93
Joint Tenancy Estate Plan · 4, 16

K

Key Advisors · 37
Key Employee Benefit Funding · 78
Key Employee Loss Coverage · 78
Key Man Insurance · 72

L

Leadership Development Program · 71
Life Insurance Trust · 16, 53, 61, 81, 82
Lifetime Estate Tax Exemption · 55
Lifetime Exemption Gifts · 16, 17
Lifetime Gift Tax Exemption · 55
Limited Liability Company · 17, 57, 59, 94, 95
Living Trust · 6, 7, 14, 15, 16, 18, 23, 24, 25, 26, 27, 28, 31, 32, 33, 34, 35, 38, 41, 54, 59, 61, 80, 84, 85, 87, 88, 89, 92, 93, 94, 95
Living Trust Estate Plan · 4, 6, 31
Long Term Care Coverage · 78
Long Term Care Insurance · 85
Long-Term Care Insurance · 94
Long-Term Care Insurance Policies · 37

M

Mortgage Payoff · 78

O

Outside Route Exit Plan · 71
Owner Blueprint · 71
Owner's Manual · 21

P

Personal Guarantees · 51
Personal Wealth Plan · 71
Probate · 4, 7, 8, 10, 26, 27, 29, 30, 33, 38, 39, 41, 45, 93, 94, 95
Probate Court · 4, 8, 16, 26, 27, 38, 41, 93

Made in the USA
Lexington, KY
08 November 2013